Dickens' Women

D1231464

Dickens' Women

Miriam Margolyes and Sonia Fraser

To the memory of our parents

Published by Hesperus Press Limited
19 Bulstrode Street, London W1U 2JN
www.hesperuspress.com

First published by Hesperus Press Limited, 2011.

Images reproduced with grateful thanks to Philip V. Allingham.

Incidental piano music for the play was arranged from contemporary sources
by Michael Haslam.

Typeset by Bookcraft Ltd, Stroud, UK
Printed and bound by CPI Group (UK) Ltd, Croydon, CR0 4YY

ISBN: 978-1-84391-351-1

Contents

Miriam Margolyes
(Image © Branco Gaica)

Introduction

In this, his bicentenary year, it is appropriate that we should focus on Charles Dickens, the last great artist to reach and delight all classes of Society, from politicians, professors, shipping magnates and Royalty to the servants, hansom-cab drivers, farmers and navigators, whose work supported and enabled England to flourish and dominate the world in the nineteenth century. His writing, full of social observation and fierce criticism, remains as relevant as ever. And the man himself, contradictory, charming, mercurial and driven, demands our scrutiny.

We are constantly being warned against using the biographical approach to literature. I agree it can be treacherous but I defend its application to the work of Charles Dickens. More than any other writer, his life was in his work. Many biographers have written and are writing about Dickens but only one, his great friend John Forster, actually knew the man himself. It is a life worth studying in detail because of its great contrasts, its secrets and because of the genius of the subject. He is our greatest prose writer, he stands with Shakespeare as a Master, his creations are etched in our consciousness. The life started in obscurity, and then rose to the heights of wealth and celebrity. It is a romantic story of rags to riches; these always appeal to the Public. But it is also a story of committed application, focused energy and occasionally ruthless exploitation. Each time we learn of a new twist in Mr Dickens' fortune, we realise that we are dealing with a man of many contradictory facets, a man capable of deep compassion and sharp cruelty, of miserable insecurity and staggering conceit.

Oliver Twist was the first Dickens book that I read. It was *his* second book, usually a stumbling-block for writers. Not so for him. I was eleven and was immediately gripped by the story – what is going to happen next – and then by the characters, who are described so exactly that I saw them quite clearly and reacted to them emotionally. I particularly enjoyed Fagin. I am Jewish and I did resent some of the descriptions: 'as he glided stealthily along, creeping beneath the shelter of the walls and doorways, the hideous old man seemed like some loathsome reptile, engendered in the slime and darkness through which he moved: crawling forth, by night, in search of some rich offal for a meal.' But I couldn't help responding to the humour of the man too; as the novel progressed, I started to laugh as well as be horrified – and that's another of the special, I would say, unique techniques Dickens employs – to use Evil and Comedy intertwined – as with Squeers, Quilp and Heep. That facility is extremely useful in the theatre! He takes us, seemingly effortlessly, from the Saffron Hill den to the serenity of the Brownlow home, as if he'd been to both those places and knew them well. How could that be? From the beginning of my acquaintance with him, I wanted to know more about the man, explore his techniques and understand his artistic journey, which I came to realise mirrored his own journey, up and up through the English class system.

So when I first studied him at Cambridge, it was the man as much as the work which interested me. My great teachers, F.R. and Q.D. Leavis, taught me how Dickens fitted into the English novel's Great Tradition of moral clarity. And there was no doubt when reading him that you knew whose side he was on. He didn't hide or prevaricate or cheat; Good and Evil were palpable, clear and unequivocal, and I clutched onto his coattails and flew through the novels, reacting exactly as he wanted me to – with horror sometimes, as in *Oliver Twist*:

'The eyes again!' he cried in an unearthly screech. Staggering as if struck by lightning, he lost his balance and tumbled over the parapet. The noose was on his neck. It ran up with his weight, tight as a bowstring, and swift as the arrow it speeds.

He fell for five-and-thirty feet. There was a sudden jerk, a terrific convulsion of the limbs; and there he hung, with the open knife clenched in his stiffening hand.

And sometimes with laughter – this description of Mrs Gamp from *Martin Chuzzlewit*, the fifth of his novels:

She was a fat old woman, this Mrs Gamp, with a husky voice and a moist eye, which she had a remarkable power of turning up, and only showing the white of it. Having very little neck, it cost her some trouble to look over herself, if one may say so, at those to whom she talked. She wore a very rusty black gown, rather the worse for snuff, and a shawl and bonnet to correspond. In these dilapidated articles of dress she had, on principle, arrayed herself, time out of mind, on such occasions as the present; for this at once expressed a decent amount of veneration for the deceased, and invited the next of kin to present her with a fresher suit of weeds; an appeal so frequently successful, that the very fetch and ghost of Mrs Gamp, bonnet and all, might be seen hanging up, any hour in the day, in at least a dozen of the second-hand clothes shops about Holborn. The face of Mrs Gamp – the nose in particular – was somewhat red and swollen, and it was difficult to enjoy her society without becoming conscious of a smell of spirits. Like most persons who have attained to great eminence in their profession, she took to hers very kindly; insomuch that, setting aside her natural predilections as a woman, she went to a lying-in or a laying-out with equal zest and relish.

It was that description which started my thinking of myself as a possible exponent of Dickens onstage. Having very little neck myself, it seemed quite possible that I could play Mrs Gamp and use some of my unfortunate physical qualities to bring her into the theatre. She was based, as John Forster relates, on a real nurse: 'and the common habit of this nurse in the sick room, among other Gampish peculiarities, was to rub her nose along the top of the tall fender'. Dickens knew he was creating an icon; he wrote to Forster: 'I mean to make a mark with her'. And he did.

The world of 1812 into which Dickens was born, was very unlike our own time and indeed, quite unlike the year in which he died, 1870. Dickens was born a Georgian, into the brutal, colourful world of the stagecoach and the Riot, when most people lived in the country, stayed there and knew their place. But it was the beginning of a great change in the world. When he was thirteen, the Stockton and Darlington Railway opened and became the first of many to provide a new form of transport across the nation, when Dickens was twenty-five, a giddy, passionate young girl of strict morals and German upbringing ascended the throne; and in 1870, the year of his death, convict transportation to Australia ceased.

All these events were part of a shift in the social order. As the changes were happening, Dickens lived through them, watched them and recorded the England he saw.

Social class has always been the crux of English comedy and Dickens, so acutely self-aware from his earliest days in the blacking factory, was always measuring himself on the social graph. His characters reflect those minute gradations of class distinction peculiar to the English and our picture of the world of Dickens' time is largely built from the observations of fiction. Because Dickens' own experience travelled up and down the social scale, likewise his characters reflect and occupy the complete and vivid tapestry of this changing social order.

His competence as a writer, quite aside from his genius, springs from his apprenticeship as a journalist. He loved reading and at eighteen he got his Reader's Ticket to the British Museum. At this time he was working as a reporter in the

Law Courts, where he would have seen a variety of desperate, poverty-stricken and damaged people; they feature most strongly in *Bleak House*. Miss Flite's tragedy, with which we end our script, combines Dickens' compassion with the accuracy of his reporter's eye. Dickens defends in his Preface the truth of his words:

> In this connexion, I mention here that everything set forth in these pages concerning the Court of Chancery is substantially true, and within the truth. The case of Gridley is in no essential altered from one of actual occurrence, made public by a disinterested person who was professionally acquainted with the whole of the monstrous wrong from beginning to end. At the present moment (August, 1853) there is a suit before the court which was commenced nearly twenty years ago, in which from thirty to forty counsel have been known to appear at one time, in which costs have been incurred to the amount of seventy thousand pounds, which is A FRIENDLY SUIT, and which is (I am assured) no nearer to its termination now than when it was begun. There is another well-known suit in Chancery, not yet decided, which was commenced before the close of the last century and in which more than double the amount of seventy thousand pounds has been swallowed up in costs. If I wanted other authorities for Jarndyce and Jarndyce, I could rain them on these pages, to the shame of – a parsimonious public.

Dickens tried to use and manipulate the Press, in a manner that is strangely and unpleasantly familiar to us now. He trained as a journalist at the *Morning Chronicle*, earning a weekly salary of five guineas, a secure income. But journalism did not satisfy his creative energy and from the dry accuracy of his court and parliamentary pieces, he moved to creative 'sketches' which became his first published book, *Sketches By Boz*, in 1836, the year of his marriage. At the end of that marriage, which lasted for twenty-one years, his attempt to use the Press to keep the public on his side was a rare mistake in the reading of Public Opinion.

There is no doubt that Dickens' creative power was equally at home creating men and women. Michael Slater, in his brilliant book *Dickens and Women*, has divided the women into three groups: the unattainable sexual object, the pre-pubescent, idealised woman and the grotesque who was both comic and frightening.

But there was an important gap in his repertoire of females. I would argue that he never portrayed a woman whom we would recognise as a mature sexual and emotional partner for his heroes. And I venture to suggest this was because his own relations with women were all damaged, incomplete or destructive. As his daughter, Kate Perugini, remarked: 'my father never understood women'.

Dickens' dark note of bitterness, resentment and a sense of injustice, which purveyed his attitude towards the female, was rooted in his relationship with his mother. He explains in the 'Autobiographical Fragment' how she was prepared to return him to the horrors of the blacking factory. I wish to quote from this piece fully because it explains so much of the man in his own words, which were read in his lifetime only by John Forster, his biographer.

> This speculation was a rivalry of 'Warren's Blacking, 30, Strand', – at that time very famous. One Jonathan Warren (the famous one was Robert), living at 30, Hungerford Stairs, or Market, Strand (for I forget which it was called then), claimed to have been the original inventor or proprietor of the blacking recipe, and to have been deposed and ill-used by his renowned relation. At last he put himself

in the way of selling his recipe, and his name, and his 30, Hungerford Stairs, Strand (30, Strand, very large, and the intermediate direction very small), for an annuity; and he set forth by his agents that a little capital would make a great business of it. The man of some property was found in George Lamert, the cousin and brother-in-law of James. He bought this right and title, and went into the blacking business and the blacking premises.

– In an evil hour for me, as I often bitterly thought. Its chief manager, James Lamert, the relative who had lived with us in Bayham Street, seeing how I was employed from day to day, and knowing what our domestic circumstances then were, proposed that I should go into the blacking warehouse, to be as useful as I could, at a salary, I think, of six shillings a week. I am not clear whether it was six or seven. I am inclined to believe, from my uncertainty on this head, that it was six at first, and seven afterwards. At any rate the offer was accepted very willingly by my father and mother, and on a Monday morning I went down to the blacking warehouse to begin my business life.

It is wonderful to me how I could have been so easily cast away at such an age. It is wonderful to me, that, even after my descent into the poor little drudge I had been since we came to London, no one had compassion enough on me – a child of singular abilities, quick, eager, delicate, and soon hurt, bodily or mentally – to suggest that something might have been spared, as certainly it might have been, to place me at any common school. Our friends, I take it, were tired out. No one made any sign. My father and mother were quite satisfied. They could hardly have been more so, if I had been twenty years of age, distinguished at a grammar school, and going to Cambridge.

The blacking warehouse was the last house on the left-hand side of the way, at old Hungerford Stairs. It was a crazy, tumbledown old house, abutting of course on the river, and literally overrun with rats. Its wainscotted rooms and its rotten floors and staircase, and the old grey rats swarming down in the cellars, and the sound of their squeaking and scuffling coming up the stairs at all times, and the dirt and decay of the place, rise up visibly before me, as if I were there again. The counting-house was on the first floor, looking over the coal-barges and the river. There was a recess in it, in which I was to sit and work. My work was to cover the pots of paste-blacking; first with a piece of oil-paper, and then with a piece of blue paper; to tie them round with a string; and then to clip the paper close and neat, all round, until it looked as smart as a pot of ointment from an apothecary's shop. When a certain number of grosses of pots had attained this pitch of perfection, I was to paste on each a printed label; and then go on again with more pots. Two or three other boys were kept at similar duty downstairs on similar wages. One of them came up, in a ragged apron and a paper cap, on the first Monday morning, to show me the trick of using the string and tying the knot. His name was Bob Fagin; and I took the liberty of using his name, long afterwards, in *Oliver Twist*.

Our relative had kindly arranged to teach me something in the dinner-hour; from twelve to one, I think it was; every day. But an arrangement so incompatible with counting-house business soon died away, from no fault of his or mine; and for the same reason, my small work-table, and my grosses of pots, my papers string, scissors, paste-pot, and labels, by little and little, vanished out of the recess in the counting-house, and kept company with the other small work-tables, grosses of pots, papers, string, scissors, and paste-pots, downstairs. It was not long, before Bob Fagin and I, and another boy whose name was Paul Green, but who was currently believed to have been christened Poll (a belief which I transferred, long after-wards again, to Mr Sweedlepipe, in *Martin Chuzzlewit*), worked generally, side by side. Bob Fagin was an orphan, and lived with his brother-in-law, a waterman. Poll Green's father had the additional distinction of being a fireman, and was employed at Drury Lane theatre; where another relation of Poll's, I think his little sister, did imps in the pantomimes.

No words can express the secret agony of my soul as I sunk into this companionship; compared these every day associates with those of my happier childhood; and felt my early hopes of growing up to be a learned and distinguished man, crushed in my breast. The deep remembrance of the sense I had of being utterly neglected and hopeless; of the shame I felt in my position; of the misery it was to my young heart to believe that, day by day, what I had learned, and thought, and delighted in, and raised my fancy and my emulation up by, was passing away from me, never to be brought back any more; cannot be written. My whole nature was so penetrated with the grief and humiliation of such considerations, that even now, famous and caressed and happy, I often forget in my dreams that I have a dear wife and children; even that I am a man; and wander deso-lately back to that time of my life.

My mother and my brothers and sisters (excepting Fanny in the royal academy of music) were still encamped, with a young servant-girl from Chatham Workhouse, in the two parlours in the emptied house in Gower Street North. It was a long way to go and return within the dinner-hour, and, usually, I either carried my dinner with me, or went and bought it at some neighbouring shop. In the latter case, it was commonly a saveloy and a penny loaf; sometimes, a four-penny plate of beef from a cook's shop; sometimes, a plate of bread and cheese, and a glass of beer, from a miserable old public-house over the way: the Swan, if I remember right, or the Swan and something else that I have forgotten. Once, I remember tucking my own bread (which I had brought from home in the morning) under my arm, wrapped up in a piece of paper like a book, and going into the best dining-room in Johnson's alamode beef-house in Clare Court, Drury Lane, and magnificently ordering a small plate of alamode beef to eat with it. What the waiter thought of such a strange little apparition, coming in all alone, I don't know; but I can see him now, staring at me as I ate my dinner, and bringing up the other waiter to look. I gave him a halfpenny, and I wish, now, that he hadn't taken it.

There is something naked and pained in that account which strikes at the heart of the man. At his core, he felt betrayed by the very women whom he most trusted, his mother, his first love, Maria Beadnell, his wife, and perhaps even by his mistress, Ellen Ternan, with whom he conducted a relationship for twelve years from 1857 to his death in 1870.

Out of that hurt and sense of abandonment came vivid and crafted characters; again and again he returned to the depiction of women who led men on and let them down; they haunt his books and their chiselled cruelty both convinces and disgusts. It's not a complete portrait of the female sex but it is a damning one.

Dickens repeated in his portraits of women these stereotypical archetypes – the pre-pubescent child, usually described as 'little' (Emily, Nell, Dorrit, Dora, Ruth Pinch); the unattainable sexual object (Estella, Lady Dedlock, Edith Dombey); the grotesque, sometimes evil (Madame Defarge, Mrs Squeers), sometimes comic (Mrs Gamp, Mrs Corney); the bad and incompetent mother (Mrs Clennam, Mrs Nickleby); the spinster longing for a man (Rosa Dartle, Miss Tox), but never was he able to draw a complete, believable, fully realised female – because the women in his life never offered him the opportunity.

Dombey and Son contains two remarkable female portraits, both of women trained, like Estella, to ensnare men; it's worth comparing Alice Marwood and Edith Dombey.

Alice got up, took off her wet cloak, and laid it aside. That done, she sat down as before, and with her arms folded, and her eyes gazing at the fire, remained silently listening with a contemptuous face to her old mother's inarticulate complainings.

'Did you expect to see me return as youthful as I went away, mother?' she said at length, turning her eyes upon the old woman. 'Did you think a foreign life, like mine, was good for good looks? One would believe so, to hear you!'

'It an't that!' cried the mother. 'She knows it!'

'What is it then?' returned the daughter. 'It had best be something that don't last, mother, or my way out is easier than my way in.'

'Hear that!' exclaimed the mother. 'After all these years she threatens to desert me in the moment of her coming back again!'

'I tell you, mother, for the second time, there have been years for me as well as you,' said Alice. 'Come back harder? Of course I have come back harder. What else did you expect?'

'Harder to me! To her own dear mother!' cried the old woman.

'I don't know who began to harden me, if my own dear mother didn't,' she returned, sitting with her folded arms, and knitted brows, and compressed lips as if she were bent on excluding, by force, every softer feeling from her breast. 'Listen, mother, to a word or two. If we understand each other now, we shall not fall out any more, perhaps. I went away a girl, and have come back a woman. I went away undutiful enough, and have come back not better, you may swear. But have you been very dutiful to me?'

'I!' cried the old woman. 'To my gal! A mother dutiful to her own child!'

'It sounds unnatural, don't it?' returned the daughter, looking coldly on her with her stern, regardless, hardy, beautiful face; 'but I have thought of it sometimes, in the course of my lone years, till I have got used to it. I have heard some talk about duty first and last; but it has always been of my duty to other people. I have wondered now and then – to pass away the time – whether no one ever owed any duty to me.'

Dickens' favourite and most autobiographical novel was *David Copperfield*. It's interesting to note that this was the book that the young Sigmund Freud gave to his fiancée.

Luckily, Dickens could never have read Freud, whose *Interpretation of Dreams* was published twenty-nine years after Dickens' death, indeed I doubt if he would have written a line if he had read him, but there is a psychological truth in Alice's character, which convinces despite the somewhat melodramatic language. It has its own reality.

The second relationship, which parallels Alice Marwood's and her mother's, is that between Edith Dombey and her mother, the truly grotesque Mrs Skewton, one of Dickens' most shocking descriptions:

At night, she should have been a skeleton, with dart and hour-glass, rather than a woman, this attendant; for her touch was as the touch of Death. The painted object shrivelled underneath her hand; the form collapsed, the hair dropped off, the arched dark eyebrows changed to scanty tufts of grey; the pale lips shrunk, the skin became cadaverous and loose; an old, worn, yellow, nodding woman, with red eyes, alone remained in Cleopatra's place, huddled up, like a slovenly bundle, in a greasy flannel gown.

Relish the passion in this confrontation between Edith and 'Cleopatra':

'Why don't you tell me,' it said sharply, 'that he is coming here to-morrow by appointment?'

'Because you know it,' returned Edith, 'Mother.'

The mocking emphasis she laid on that one word!

'You know he has bought me,' she resumed. 'Or that he will, to-morrow. He has considered of his bargain; he has shown it to his friend; he is even rather proud of it; he thinks that it will suit him, and may be had sufficiently cheap; and he will buy to-morrow. God, that I have lived for this, and that I feel it!'

Compress into one handsome face the conscious self-abasement, and the burning indignation of a hundred women, strong in passion and in pride; and there it hid itself with two white shuddering arms.

'What do you mean?' returned the angry mother. 'Haven't you from a child –'

'A child!' said Edith, looking at her, 'when was I a child? What childhood did you ever leave to me? I was a woman – artful, designing, mercenary, laying snares for men – before I knew myself, or you, or even understood the base and wretched aim of every new display I learnt. You gave birth to a woman. Look upon her. She is in her pride to-night.'

And as she spoke, she struck her hand upon her beautiful bosom, as though she would have beaten down herself.

'Look at me,' she said, 'who have never known what it is to have an honest heart, and love. Look at me, taught to scheme and plot when children play; and married in my youth – an old age of design – to one for whom I had no feeling but indifference. Look at me, whom he left a widow, dying before his inheritance descended to him – a

19

judgment on you! well deserved! – and tell me what has been my life for ten years since.'

'We have been making every effort to endeavour to secure to you a good establishment,' rejoined her mother. 'That has been your life. And now you have got it.'

'There is no slave in a market; there is no horse in a fair: so shown and offered and examined and paraded, mother, as I have been, for ten shameful years,' cried Edith, with a burning brow, and the same bitter emphasis on the one word. 'Is it not so? Have I been made the bye-word of all kinds of men? Have fools, have profligates, have boys, have dotards, dangled after me, and one by one rejected me, and fallen off, because you were too plain with all your cunning: yes, and too true, with all those false pretences: until we have almost come to be notorious? The licence of look and touch,' she said, with flashing eyes, 'have I submitted to it, in half the places of resort upon the map of England. Have I been hawked and vended here and there until the last grain of self-respect is dead within me, and I loathe myself? Has this been my late childhood? I had none before. Do not tell me that I had, to-night, of all nights in my life!'

'You might have been well married,' said her mother, 'twenty times at least, Edith, if you had given encouragement enough.'

'No! Who takes me, refuse that I am, and as I well deserve to be,' she answered, raising her head, and trembling in her energy of shame and stormy pride, 'shall take me, as this man does, with no art of mine put forth to lure him. He sees me at the auction, and he thinks it well to buy me. Let him! When he came to view me – perhaps to bid – he required to see the roll of my accomplishments. I gave it to him. When he would have me show one of them, to justify his purchase to his men, I require of him to say which he demands, and I exhibit it. I will do no more. He makes the purchase of his own will, and with his own sense of its worth, and the power of his money; and I hope it may never disappoint him. I have not vaunted and pressed the bargain; neither have you, so far as I have been able to prevent you.'

'You talk strangely to-night, Edith, to your own mother.'

'It seems so to me; stranger to me than you,' said Edith. 'But my education was completed long ago. I am too old now, and have fallen too low, by degrees, to take a new course, and to stop yours, and to help myself. The germ of all that purifies a woman's breast, and makes it true and good, has never stirred in mine, and I have nothing else to sustain me when I despise myself.' There had been a touching sadness in her voice, but it was gone, when she went on to say, with a curled lip, 'So, as we are genteel and poor, I am content that we should be made rich by these means; all I say is, I have kept the only purpose I have had the strength to form – I had almost said the power, with you at my side, mother – and have not tempted this man on.'

'This man! You speak,' said her mother, 'as if you hated him.'

'And you thought I loved him, did you not?' she answered, stopping on her way across the room, and looking round. 'Shall I tell you,' she continued, with her eyes fixed on her mother, 'who already knows us thoroughly, and reads us right, and before whom I have even less of self-respect or confidence than before my own inward self; being so much degraded by his knowledge of me?'

… Edith suddenly let fall her face, as if it had been stung, and while she pressed her hands upon it, a terrible tremble crept over her whole frame. It was quickly gone; and with her usual step, she passed out of the room.

The maid who should have been a skeleton, then reappeared, and giving one arm to her mistress, who appeared to have taken off her manner with her charms, and to have put on paralysis with her flannel gown, collected the ashes of Cleopatra, and carried them away in the other, ready for tomorrow's revivification.

In the piece of Mrs Skewton which I chose for *Dickens' Women*, I have used the comic portrayal and only at the end of the excerpt do I show the disgust which Dickens always felt about women who should have been past the age of Lust but still burned with longing for Man. Maria Winter, née Beadnell, was the progenitor of many such sad creatures.

Despite the damage Dickens sustained from women, or perhaps because of it, his creativity flourished and he forces us into the 'Dickens world', which is perhaps not an entirely realistic one but which nonetheless convinces, enthrals and moves us with its emotional power.

Here is the young Pip suffering an encounter with Estella:

> She gave me a triumphant glance in passing me, as if she rejoiced that my hands were so coarse and my boots were so thick, and she opened the gate, and stood holding it. I was passing out without looking at her, when she touched me with a taunting hand. 'Why don't you cry?' 'Because I don't want to.' 'You do,' said she. 'You have been crying till you are half blind, and you are near crying again now.' She laughed contemptuously, pushed me out, and locked the gate upon me.

One of the most interesting pieces of research we did in preparing the script was in discovering the story, so well-hidden for many years, of Dickens' adultery and his dismissal of his wife in 1857. Now, the full story of the divorce has been told in both Claire Tomalin's book, *The Invisible Woman*, and in Lillian Nayder's, *The Other Dickens*, but in 1989 when our show came to the Edinburgh Festival, few knew the extent of Dickens' brutality to Catherine and the lengths to which he was prepared to go, both to keep his reputation secure and to continue his relationship with his mistress, Ellen Ternan. In the script, Catherine's story was heard for the first time. It seems to me that Dickens followed the known pattern of the abused becoming the abuser; I cannot forgive him.

He wrote two letters, one to John Forster and one to Baroness Burdett-Coutts, both letters a tissue of self-serving lies.

John Forster, 3rd Sept 1857

Poor Catherine and I are not made for each other, and there is no help for it. It is not only that she makes me uneasy and unhappy, but that I make her so too – and much more so. She is exactly what you know, in the way of being amiable and complying; but we are strangely ill-assorted for the bond there is between us. God knows she would have been a thousand times happier if she had married another kind of man, and that her avoidance of this destiny would have been at least equally good for us both. I am often cut to the heart by thinking what a pity it is, for her own sake, that I ever fell in her way; and if I were sick or disabled to-morrow, I know how sorry she would be, and how deeply grieved myself, to think how we had lost each other. But exactly the same incompatibility would arise, the moment I was well again; and nothing on earth could make her understand me, or suit us to each other. Her temperament will not go with mine.

It mattered not so much when we had only ourselves to consider, but reasons have been growing since which make it all but hopeless that we should even try to struggle on. What is now befalling me I have seen steadily coming, ever since the days you remember when Mary was born; and I know too well that you cannot, and no one can, help me. Why I have even written I

23

hardly know; but it is a miserable sort of comfort that you should be clearly aware how matters stand. The mere mention of the fact, without any complaint or blame of any sort, is a relief to my present state of spirits – and I can get this only from you, because I can speak of it to no one else.

Baroness Burdett-Coutts, 9th May 1858

... if the children loved her, or had ever loved her, this severance would have been a far easier thing than it is. But she has never attached one of them to herself, never played with them in their infancy, never attracted their confidence as they have grown older, never presented herself before them in the aspect of a mother.

That is the story Dickens wanted heard, his interpretation of the breakdown of the marriage. He would go to any lengths to keep the truth from his Public: that he had made his wife pregnant twelve times, that he had grown tired of her and had been joyously inflamed by a younger, slenderer woman.

But, of course, there is the other Dickens, the jolly man more familiar to the public, and I would be doing Dickens a disservice if I omitted the humour for which he is justly famous. Here are two gems I relish, examples of the smaller characters he would so expertly give life to. In the first, from *Martin Chuzzlewit* (1843–44), the landlady, Mrs Todgers, talks to the Pecksniff daughters.

'Presiding over an establishment like this, makes sad havoc with the features, my dear Miss Pecksniffs,' said Mrs Todgers. 'The gravy alone, is enough to add twenty years to one's age, I do assure you.'

'Lor!' cried the two Miss Pecksniffs.

'The anxiety of that one item, my dears,' said Mrs Todgers, 'keeps the mind continually upon the stretch.

There is no such passion in human nature, as the passion for gravy among commercial gentlemen. It's nothing to say a joint won't yield – a whole animal wouldn't yield – the amount of gravy they expect each day at dinner. And what I have undergone in consequence,' cried Mrs Todgers, raising her eyes and shaking her head, 'no one would believe!'

And the glorious Mrs Wititterley in *Nicholas Nickleby*, from a higher class but equally hilarious:

'I take an interest, my lord,' said Mrs Wititterly, with a faint smile, 'such an interest in the drama.'

'Ye-es. It's very interesting,' replied Lord Verisopht.

'I'm always ill after Shakespeare,' said Mrs Wititterly. 'I scarcely exist the next day; I find the reaction so very great after a tragedy, my lord, and Shakespeare is such a delicious creature.'

'Ye-es!' replied Lord Verisopht. 'He was a clayver man.'

'Do you know, my lord,' said Mrs Wititterly, after a long silence, 'I find I take so much more interest in his plays, after having been to that dear little dull house he was born in! Were you ever there, my lord?'

'No, nayver,' replied Verisopht.

'Then really you ought to go, my lord,' returned Mrs Wititterly, in very languid and drawling accents. 'I don't know how it is, but after you've seen the place and written your name in the little book, somehow or other you seem to be inspired; it kindles up quite a fire within one.'

I am convinced that the way to read Dickens is to read him aloud, just as Dickens himself did when he wrote standing at his desk, wiping his eyes with laughter, then running to the mirror to practise his faces and weeping as he killed off Little Nell.

John Forster writes in his Biography: 'he is said on one occasion to have declared to the critic that every word uttered by his characters was distinctly *heard* by him before it was written down'.

Dickens makes it easy to find the voices for his characters; Mrs Gamp's dialogue, for example, is written using the letter 'g' instead of 's' so I knew exactly how to pronounce 'when I am so dispoged' and could gauge the level of drunkenness to employ for this vicious, sublime creation. Mrs Micawber's voice surprised me. She is often presented unsympathetically, being both harsh and stupid, but I heard her as an anxious woman, desperately searching for gentility and public recognition of her pre-marital status. The piece in the script is quite touching; often I could hear the audience weeping as I said 'I never will'.

I am brave enough to present three males in the show – Pip, Towlinson and Mr Bumble. Mr Bumble pushed his way into the show and I have to admit he is enormous fun to play. The combination of amorousness and cupidity which Dickens so brilliantly displays in the scene with the teaspoons gave me the unctuous voice for this obese predator.

I hope, as you read the script of *Dickens' Women*, you will enjoy Flora Finching, Mrs Corney and all the others as much as I enjoy performing them and perhaps will find a voice for them yourselves.

Charles Dickens

Elizabeth Dickens – Charles Dickens' mother

Catherine Dickens – Charles Dickens' wife

Ellen Ternan – Charles Dickens' mistress

Dickens' Women

'I'm coming. Is it Mrs Perkins? What, Mr Whilks! Don't say it's you, Mr Whilks, and that poor creeture Mrs Whilks with not even a pincushion ready. Don't say it's you, Mr Whilks! And so the gentleman's dead, sir! Ah! The more's the pity. But it's what we must all come to. It's as certain as being born, except that we can't make our calculations as exact. Ah! Poor dear!

'Ah dear! When Gamp was summonsed to his long home, and I see him a lying in the hospital with a penny-piece on each eye, and his wooden leg under his left arm, I thought I should have fainted away. But I bore up. If it wasn't for the nerve a little sip of liquor gives me I never could go through with what I sometimes has to do.

'"Mrs Harris," I says to my friend Mrs Harris at the very last case as ever I acted in, which it was but a young person, – "Mrs Harris," I says, "leave the bottle on the chimley-piece, and don't ask me to take none, but let me put my lips to it when I am so dispoged, and then I will do what I am engaged to do, according to the best of my ability."

'"Mrs Gamp," she says in answer, "if ever there was a sober creeture to be got at eighteen-pence a day for working people, and three and six for gentlefolks – night-watching being a extra charge – you are that inwallable person."

'"Mrs Harris," I says to her, "don't name the charge, for if I could afford to lay all my fellow-creeturs out for nothink, I would gladly do it, sich is the love I bears 'em."

'Thank you sir. How are you Mr Mould? Everything be nice and comfortable about the deceased. You know me of old, I hope, and so does Mrs Mould, your 'andsome pardner sir and so does the two sweet, young ladies, your darters; although the blessing of a daughter was deniged myself, which if we had one, Gamp would certainly have drunk its little shoes right off its feet.

'But them two sweet, young ladies of yourn, Mr Mould, as I knowed afore a tooth in their pretty heads was cut, and have many a time seen – ah! the dear creeturs! a-playing at berryins down in the shop and a-follerin' the order-book to its long home in the iron safe. Young ladies with such faces as your darters thinks of somethin' else besides berryins'; don't they, sir? Thinks o' marryin's; don't they, sir?

'You ought to know that you was born in a wale, and that you live in a wale, and that you must take the consequences of sich a sitivation.

'I takes new bread, my dear, with jest a little pat o' fredge butter and a morsel o' cheese: and whatever you do, young woman, don't bring me more than a shillingsworth of gin-and-water, when I rings the bell a second time; for that is always my allowange, and I never takes a drop beyond.

'Rich folk may ride on camels, but it ain't so easy for them to see out of a needle's eye. That is my comfort and I hopes I knows it. Drat the old wexagious creetur, I a'most forgot your piller, I declare! There! Now you're as comfortable as you need to be, I'm sure! and I'm going to be comfortable too.'

[*Seated in the chair asleep. Opens eyes.*]

That was Mrs Gamp from *Martin Chuzzlewit*, and I am Miriam Margolyes from Clapham.

Mr Mould the undertaker was a great admirer of Mrs Gamp. He said she was 'the sort of woman you would bury for nothing and do it neatly'.

I've had a passion for Dickens all my life. I learnt from him that literature is not peripheral to life: it is the stuff of life itself. Dickens distilled his life's experience into the most marvellous essence and particularly the women in his life fuelled the women in his books. I want to share with you my relish in their humour, their variety, their vitality. Everybody thinks of Dickens as

30

Mrs Gamp – Fred Barnard, 1879

the warm, jolly, family man, the *paterfamilias*, the inventor of Christmas. 'God Bless us every one,' says Tiny Tim.

[*Music under.*]

But there was a tormented, demonic side to his nature that had its roots in the darkness of his childhood.

Kate Perugini, his favourite daughter, wrote to George Bernard Shaw, 'If you could make the public understand that my father was not a jolly, jocose gentleman walking about the earth with a plum pudding and a bowl of punch, you would greatly oblige me.' I want to oblige Kate tonight.

Dickens could write about the gripe of poverty, about people living on the underbelly of life, on the edge of existence because he had been there himself.

Do you know the Klems from *The Uncommercial Traveller*?

I am waited on by an elderly woman with a chronic sniff, who, at the shadowy hour of half past nine o'clock of every evening, gives admittance at the street door to a meagre and mouldy old man whom I have never yet seen detached from a flat pint of beer in a pewter pot.

The meagre and mouldy old man is her husband, and the pair have a dejected consciousness that they are not justified in appearing on the surface of the earth.

They come out of some nook when London empties itself and go in again when it fills. They make their bed in the lowest and remotest corner of the basement and they smell of bed, and have no possessions but bed: unless it be (which I rather gather from an undercurrent of flavour on them) cheese.

The most extraordinary circumstance I have traced in connection with this aged couple is that there is a Miss Klem, their daughter, apparently ten years older than either of them, who also has a bed and smells of it, and carries it about the earth at dusk and hides it in deserted houses.

I came into this piece of knowledge through Mrs Klem's beseeching me to sanction the sheltering of Miss Klem under that roof for a single night, 'between her takin' care of the upper part in Pall Mall which the family of his back, and a 'ouse in Serjameses-Street, which the family of leaves town ter-morrer'.

I gave my gracious consent, and in the shadowy hours Miss Klem became perceptible on the doorstep wrestling with a bed in a bundle. Where she made it up for the night I cannot positively state, but I think in a sink. I know that with the instinct of a reptile or insect, she stowed it and herself away in deep obscurity.

[*Music.*]

This vaguely ecclesiastical structure is a copy of Dickens' own reading desk, which he designed himself and toured with all over England and America with his dramatic readings. These were immensely successful: in 1868, when he went to New York, over 25,000 people came to hear him, and he made far more money out of his readings than he ever did out of his writings.

I suppose most people's view of a typical Dickens heroine is somebody like Pet Meagles from *Little Dorrit*. 'Pet was about twenty. A fair girl with rich brown hair hanging free in natural ringlets. A lovely girl, with a frank face, and wonderful eyes; so large, so soft, so bright, set to perfection in her kind, good head. She was round and fresh and dimpled and spoilt, and there was in Pet an air of timidity and dependence which was the best weakness in the world.'

[*Music.*]

And then there's Kate Nickleby from *Nicholas Nickleby*:

'A slight but very beautiful and gentle girl of about seventeen.'

Mary Graham (from *Martin Chuzzlewit*), no more than seventeen, her figure slight as became her years but all the charms of youth and maidenhood clustered on her gentle brow.

Ada Clare (from *Bleak House*), with the fire shining on her, a beautiful girl of seventeen with such soft, blue eyes and such a bright, innocent, and trusting face.

And Alice (from *The Sisters of York*), a fair creature of seventeen. The heart of this fair girl bounded with youth and gladness, her gleesome voice and merry laughs were the sweetest music of their home. She was its very light and life.

[*End music.*]

Have you noticed they're all about seventeen? That is because they were all based on Mary Hogarth, Dickens' young sister-in-law, who came to live with Dickens and his wife Catherine when they were first married. And the important thing to remember about Mary is that she died… at seventeen. They had been to the St James's theatre together – all three of them: Dickens loved to go out with a sister on each arm; he called them 'my pair of petticoats, my two Venuses', and they'd come home, happy and laughing; Mary had gone upstairs to take off her cloak, Dickens was walking upstairs behind her and suddenly she fell back into his arms – and died.

He had a pathological attachment to her: he wrote, 'her last words were of me. I have lost the dearest friend I ever had… she had not a single fault and was in life almost as far above the foibles and vanity of her sex and age as she is now in Heaven.'

He wanted to be buried in the same grave with her, and was most upset when her younger brother died first and was buried there instead.

'It is a great trial to me to give up Mary's grave, greater than I can express. I thought of having her moved to the catacombs and saying nothing about it… I cannot bear the thought of being parted from her dust.'

He composed the epitaph for her tombstone in Kensal Green cemetery, 'Young, beautiful, and good, God numbered her with his angels at the tender age of seventeen,' and she became in his writing the pregenitor of all those tiny, little, pre-pubescent, mini-breasted, child love-objects, like Dora, Ruth Pinch, Little Dorrit, Florence Dombey, Little Em'ly, and of course the most famous of all, Little Nell. I find them all rather icky, actually. So did Oscar Wilde.

He wrote: 'One would have to have a heart of stone to read the death of Little Nell without laughing… '

And G.K. Chesterton, a brilliant Dickens commentator, wrote: 'Around Little Nell, of course, a controversy raged and rages. Some implored Dickens not to kill her at the end of the story. Some regret that he did not kill her at the beginning.'

So I thought it would be nice to show Little Nell having some fun for a change (before she died) with Mrs Jarley, the owner of the Waxworks, from *The Old Curiosity Shop*.

[*Music.*]

Mrs Jarley: *The Old Curiosity Shop*

'There, child, read that.'

Nell walked round and read aloud the inscription, in enormous black letters, JARLEY'S WAX WORK.

'I never saw any wax-work, ma'am,' said Nell. 'Is it funnier than Punch?'

'Funnier!' said Mrs Jarley in a shrill voice. 'It is not funny at all.'

'Oh!' said Nell, with all possible humility.

'It isn't funny at all,' repeated Mrs Jarley.

'It's calm and – what's that word again – critical? – no – clas-sical, that's it – it's calm and classical. No low beatings and knockings about, no jokings and squeakings like your precious Punches, but always the same, with a constantly unchanging air of coldness and gentility; and so like life, that if wax-work only spoke and walked about, you'd hardly know the difference.

'I won't go so far as to say, that, as it is, I've seen wax-work quite like life, but I've certainly seen some life that was exactly like wax-work.

'That, ladies and gentlemen, is Jasper Packlemerton of atrocious memory, who courted and married fourteen wives and destroyed them all by tickling the soles of their feet when they was sleeping in the consciousness of innocence and virtue.

'On being brought to the scaffold and asked if he was sorry for what he had done, he replied yes, he was sorry for having let 'em off so easy and hoped all Christian husbands would pardon him the offence.

'Let this be a warning to all young ladies to be particular in the character of the gentlemen of their choice.

'Observe that his fingers is curled as if in the act of tickling, and that his face is represented with a wink, as he appeared when committing his barbarous murders.'

When Nell knew all about Mr Packlemerton and could say it without faltering, Mrs Jarley passed on to the fat man, and then to the thin man, the tall man, the short man, the old lady who died of dancing at a hundred and thirty-two, the wild boy of the woods, the woman who poisoned fourteen families with pickled walnuts, and other historical characters and interesting but misguided individuals.

'Finally, that,' said Mrs Jarley, 'is an unfortunate Maid of Honour in the time of Queen Elizabeth, who died from pricking her finger in consequence of working upon a Sunday.

'Observe the blood which is trickling from her finger; also the gold-eyed needle of the period with which she is at work.'

[*Music.*]

Dickens came from the lower middle class and he hated it. The anatomy of our English class system is such that the lower middle class is probably the worst class to be born into – because it lacks both the dignity of the working class and the confidence, the security of the middle class and anyone who has the misfortune to be born into the lower middle class can spend a lifetime trying to claw their way out of it... Dickens was a passionate and a determined and ultimately a successful social climber.

But his childhood was shrouded in debt and disgrace. His grandfather was forced to flee to France because he was caught embezzling the funds of the Navy pay office where he worked and his father John Dickens (he wasn't a criminal, but he was a feckless man, hopeless with money – probably the model for Mr Micawber) was finally arrested when Dickens was twelve years old for owing the baker forty pounds. The whole family was imprisoned in the Marshalsea debtors' prison in London, all except for little Charles himself. His parents sent him quite alone to board with a Mrs Elizabeth Roylance, 'a reduced old lady, long known to our family, in Little College Street, Camden Town, who took children in to board and had done so in Brighton'. She is the inspiration for Mrs Pipchin, here confronting little Paul Dombey in *Dombey and Son*.

This celebrated Mrs Pipchin was a marvellous ill-favoured, ill-conditioned old lady, of a stooping figure, with a mottled face, like bad marble, a hook nose, and a hard grey eye, that looked as if it might have been hammered at on an anvil without sustaining any injury.

Forty years at least had elapsed since the death of Mr Pipchin; but his relict still wore black bombazeen, of such a lustreless, deep, dead, sombre shade, that gas itself couldn't light her up after dark. She was generally spoken of as 'a great manager' of children; and the secret of her management was, to give them everything they didn't like, and nothing that they did. Which was said to sweeten their dispositions very much.

'Well, Sir,' said Mrs Pipchin to Paul, 'how do you think you shall like me?'

'I don't think I shall like you at all,' replied Paul. 'I want to go away. This isn't my house.'

'No. It's mine,' retorted Mrs Pipchin.

'It's a very nasty one,' said Paul.

'There's a worse place in it than this though,' said Mrs Pipchin, 'where we shut up our bad boys,' for Mrs Pipchin always made a point of being particularly cross on Sunday nights.

And there with an aching void in his young heart, and all outside so cold, and bare, and strange, Paul sat as if he had taken life unfurnished, and the upholsterer were never coming.

[*Music.*]

Dickens saw himself for the rest of his life as a deprived child. He wrote of Florence Dombey – but really it was himself – 'not an orphan in the wide world can be so deserted as the child who is an outcast from a living parent's love.'

The core of resentment which he felt stems from his feelings about his mother. The family was always terribly poor, always struggling with debt, and Elizabeth Dickens was always fanatically trying to keep up appearances – like Mrs Micawber in *David Copperfield*:

'I never thought before I was married, when I lived with papa and mama, that I should ever find it necessary to take a lodger. But Mr Micawber being in difficulties, all considerations of private feelings must give way.

'Mr Micawber's difficulties are almost overwhelming just at present and whether it is possible to bring him through them, I don't know.

'If Mr Micawber's creditors will not give him time they must take the consequences; and the sooner they bring it to an issue the better. Blood cannot be obtained from a stone, neither can anything on account be obtained at present from Mr Micawber.

'With the exception of the heel of a Dutch cheese – which is not adapted to the wants of a young family – there is really not a scrap of anything in the larder.

'I was accustomed to speak of the larder when I lived with papa and mama, and I use the word almost unconsciously. What I mean to express is, that there is nothing to eat in the house.

'I have pawned the plate myself. Six tea, two salt, and a pair of sugars, I have at different times borrowed money on, in secret, with my own hands, and to me, with my recollections, of papa and mama, these transactions are very painful. There are still a few trifles that we could part with. Mr Micawber's feelings would never allow him to dispose of them; and Clickett being of a vulgar mind, would take painful liberties if so much confidence was reposed in her. Master Copperfield, if I might ask you... ?

'My family may consider it banishment, if they please; but I am a wife and mother, and I will never desert Mr Micawber.

'That, that is my view of the obligation which I took upon myself when I repeated the irrevocable words, "I Emma, take thee, Wilkins". I read that service over with a flat-candle on the previous night, and the conclusion I derived from it was, that I could never desert Mr Micawber.

'And though it is possible I may be mistaken in my view of the ceremony, I never will!'

Dickens is so wonderful with names. Wilkins makes it perfect.

You can see from his notebooks how Dickens arrives at the various names. Mrs Pipchin for example started off as Mrs Tipchin, then Mrs Alchin, Mrs Somechin, Mrs Pipchin.

After the family came out of the Marshalsea prison they were still desperately poor and his parents sent Dickens to work for six shillings a week, in a blacking factory at number 30, Hungerford Stairs, just off the Strand.

It was the worst time of his whole life. He could never pass by that address, for the rest of his life, without crossing the road, and he never spoke of it to anyone.

The extraordinary thing was that even as a little boy he had such a sense of himself, such a belief in his own destiny, that he felt humiliated because the passers-by could see him through the factory windows, pasting the labels on the blacking bottles.

He felt it the more keenly, because his sister Fanny had just won a scholarship to the Royal Academy of Music and while he was toiling away in the dirt, she was learning the graces of music and piano.

He had one friend there, a cheerful, carrotty-headed little boy called Bob Fagin, but he begged his parents to take him away and send him back to school.

One day, his father had a row with James Lamert, the owner of the blacking factory, and took his son away. The very next morning his mother went back to Mr Lamert, trying to persuade him to keep Dickens working. Perhaps she felt they needed the money.

Twenty years later, in an autobiographical fragment that was never published in his lifetime, he wrote of the pain of that realisation:

'I never afterwards forgot, I never shall forget, I never can forget, that my mother was warm for my being sent back.'

Despite the early days Dickens was a dutiful son. He took care of his mother financially. 'My mother was left to me when my father died. I never had anything left me but relations.' (He describes her as being 'got up in sables like a female Hamlet', and when he visited her, she would 'pluck up a spirit and asked for a pound'.)

It was different with his grandmother. She was 'in service'. She had been the housekeeper to the Earl of Crewe: Dickens loved listening to her stories when he was a little boy. Dickens draws an affectionate portrait of her as Mrs Lirriper, the lodging housekeeper from *Household Words*.

Mrs Lirriper, 1863

It was early in the second year of my married life that I lost my poor Lirriper and I set up in Islington directly afterwards and afterwards came here.

Servant girls are one of your first and one of your lasting troubles, being like your teeth which begin with convulsions and never cease tormenting you from the time you cut them till they cut you, and then you don't want to part with them which seems hard but we must succumb or buy artificial, and even where you get a will nine times out of ten you'll get a dirty face with it and naturally lodgers do not like good society to be shown in with a smear of black across the nose or a smudgy eyebrow.

Where they pick up the black is a mystery I cannot solve, as in the case of the willingest girl that ever came into a house half-starved poor thing, a girl so willing that I called her Willing Sophy down on her knees scrubbing early and late and ever cheerful but always smiling with a black face.

And I says to Sophy, 'Now Sophy my good girl have a regular day for your stoves and keep the width of the Airy between yourself and the blacking and do not brush your hair with the bottom of the saucepans and do not meddle with the snuffs of candles and it stands to reason that it can no longer be yet there it was and always on her nose, which turning up and being broad at the end seemed to boast of it and caused warning from a steady gentleman and excellent lodger (breakfast by the week, use of sitting-room when required) his words being, "Mrs Lirriper, I have arrived at the point of admitting that the Black is a man and a brother but only in a natural form and when it can't be got off."'

Well consequently I put poor Sophy on to other work and forbid her answering the door or answering a bell on any account but she was unfortunately so willing that nothing would stop her flying up the kitchen stairs whenever a bell was heard to tingle.

I put it to her: 'Oh Sophy, Sophy, for goodness, goodness sake, where does it come from?'

To which that poor, unlucky, willing mortal bursting out crying to see me so vexed replied, 'I took a deal of black into me ma'am when I was a small child, being much neglected and I think it must be that it works out.'

So it continuing to work out of that poor thing and not having another fault to find with her I says 'Sophy what do you seriously think of my helping you away to New South Wales where it might not be noticed?'

Nor did I ever repent the money which was well spent, for she married the ship's cook on the voyage (himself a Mulateer) and did well and lived happy and so far as I ever heard it was not noticed in a new state of society to her dying day.

[*Music.*]

When Dickens was eighteen, and working as a reporter in the Houses of Parliament, he fell wildly and passionately and explosively in love with a frivolous young woman called Maria Beadnell.

David Copperfield meeting Dora Spenlow is Charles Dickens meeting Maria Beadnell.

All was over in a moment. I had fulfilled my destiny. I was a captive and a slave. I loved Dora Spenlow to distraction!

She was more than a human to me. She was a Fairy, a Sylph, I don't know what she was – anything that no one ever saw, and everything that everybody ever wanted.

I don't remember who was there, except Dora. I have not the least idea what we had for dinner, besides Dora. My impression is, that I dined off Dora entirely, and sent away half-a-dozen plates untouched. I sat next to her. I talked to her. She had the most delightful little voice, the gayest little laugh, the pleasantest and most fascinating little ways, that ever led a lost youth into hopeless slavery.

But to Dickens' despair, Maria's parents were dead against the match. They didn't want their daughter affianced to a young man without prospects – a debtor's son. And Maria herself was very wicked: she led him on, and teased him, and then she spurned him – calling him a mere boy. Boy. B.O.Y.

Three letters, which he wrote, 'scorched his brain'. He never got over it. As a matter of fact, Dickens never got over anything that happened to him.

Years later he wrote to her:

But nobody can ever know with what a sad heart I resigned you, or after what struggles and what conflict. My entire devotion to you, and the wasted tenderness of those hard years which I have ever since half loved, half dreaded to recall, made so deep an impression on me that I refer to it a habit of suppression which now belongs to me, which I know is no part of my original nature, but which makes me chary of showing my affections, even to my children, except when they are very young.

In 1855, Maria came back into his life, only she wasn't called 'Beadnell' any more. She had become Mrs Henry Winter, the wife of an impoverished sawmill manager in Finsbury. Did she make a mistake!

She wrote to Charles Dickens. He was of course by now the most famous man in England. When he saw that well-remembered handwriting on the envelope, his heart flamed into a frenzy of expectation and, very naughtily, he arranged an assignation at a time when he knew his wife Catherine would not be at home.

He wrote to her:

I fancy – though you may not have thought in the old time how manfully I loved you – that you may have seen in one of my old books a faithful recollection of the passion I had for you, & may have thought that it was something to have been loved so well, and may have seen in little bits of 'Dora' touches of your old self sometimes and a grace here and there that may be revived in your little girls, years hence, for the bewilderment of some other young lover – though he will never be as in earnest as I and David Copperfield are.

They arranged to meet and, amazingly, this brilliant man, this genius, kept alive an image of Maria as she had been when he had last seen her nineteen years before. She tried to warn him in a letter that she had changed. Dickens replied:

When you say you are toothless, fat, old and ugly, which I don't believe, I fly away to the house in Lombard Street and see you in a sort of raspberry-coloured dress with little, black, Van Dykes at the top, and my boyish heart pinned like a captured butterfly to every one of them.

She arrived, nineteen years older, and shattered his dreams. He could never forgive her for having grown older and he took his literary revenge when he wrote the character of Flora Finching in *Little Dorrit*.

Flora Finching: *Little Dorrit*, 1855–57

Flora, always tall, had grown to be very broad too, and short of breath; but that was not much. Flora, whom he had left a lily, had become a peony; but that was not much. Flora, who had seemed enchanting in all she said and thought, was diffuse and silly. That was much. Flora, who had been spoiled and artless long ago, was determined to be spoiled and artless now. That was a fatal blow. This is Flora!

'I am sure I am ashamed to see Mr Clennam, I am a mere fright, I know he'll find me fearfully changed, I am actually an old

Flora Finching – Sol Eytinge, 1867

woman, it's shocking to be found out, it's really shocking.

'Oh! But with a gentleman it's so different and really you look so amazingly well that you have no right to say anything of the kind, while, as to me, you know – oh! I am dreadful!

'But if we talk of not having changed, look at papa, is not papa precisely what he was when you went away, isn't it cruel and unnatural of papa to be such a reproach to his own child, if we go on in this way much longer people who don't know us will begin to suppose that I am papa's mama!

'Oh, Mr Clennam, you insincerest of creatures, I perceive already that you have not lost your old way of paying compliments, your old way when you used to pretend to be so sentimentally struck you know – at least I don't mean that, I – oh I don't know what I mean!

'You mustn't think of going yet, you could never be so unkind as to think of going, Arthur – I mean Mr Arthur – or I suppose Mr Clennam would be far more proper – but I am sure I don't know what I am saying, but I am running into nonsense again.

'Indeed I have little doubt that you are married to some Chinese lady, being in China so long and being in business and naturally desirous to settle and extend your connection nothing was more likely than that you should propose to a Chinese lady and nothing was more natural I am sure than that the Chinese lady should accept you and think herself very well off too, I only hope she's not a Pagodian dissenter.

'Oh good gracious me I hope you never kept yourself a bachelor so long on my account! But of course you never did why should you, pray don't answer, I don't know where I'm running to, oh do tell me something about the Chinese ladies whether their eyes are really so long and narrow always putting me in mind of mother-of-pearl fish at cards, and do they really wear tails down their back and plaited too or is it only the men, and why do they stick little bells all over their bridges and temples and hats and things or don't they really do it?

46

'Then it's all true and they really do! Good gracious Arthur! – pray excuse me – old habit – Mr Clennam far more proper.

'Dear dear, only to think of the changes at home. Who could have ever imagined Mrs Finching when I can't imagine it myself!

'Finching oh yes isn't it a dreadful name, but as Mr F. said when he proposed to me he wasn't answerable for it and couldn't help it could he? Excellent man, not at all like you but excellent man!

'Romance is fled, however, as I openly said to Mr F. when he proposed to me and you will be surprised to hear that he proposed seven times once in a hackney-coach once in a boat once in a pew once on a donkey at Tunbridge Wells and the rest on his knees.

'You must know but that I have no doubt you know already, that before I was introduced to the late Mr F. I had been engaged to Arthur Clennam – we were all in all to one another, it was the morning of life, it was bliss, it was frenzy, it was everything else of that sort in the highest degree, when rent asunder we turned to stone in which capacity Arthur went to China and I became the statue bride of the late Mr F.

'Ask me not if I love him still or if he still loves me or what the end is to be or when, we are surrounded by watchful eyes and it may be that we are destined to pine asunder it may be never more to be reunited not a word not a breath not a look to betray us all must be secret as the tomb wonder not therefore that even if I should seem comparatively cold to Arthur or Arthur should seem comparatively cold to me we have fatal reasons it is enough if we understand them hush!'

Interval

Act Two

Mrs Corney and Mr Bumble: *Oliver Twist*, 1837–39

'Dear me! is that Mr Bumble?'

'At your service, ma'am,' said Mr Bumble, who had been stopping outside to rub his shoes clean, and to shake the snow off his coat; and who now made his appearance, bearing the cocked hat in one hand and a bundle in the other. 'Shall I shut the door, ma'am?'

The lady modestly hesitated to reply lest there should be any impropriety in holding an interview with Mr Bumble, with closed doors.

Mr Bumble taking advantage of the hesitation, and being very cold himself, shut it without permission.

'Hard weather, Mr Bumble.'

'Hard indeed, ma'am. Anti-parochial weather, this, ma'am. We have given away, Mrs Corney, we have given away a matter of twenty quartern loaves and a cheese and a half, this very blessed afternoon; and yet them paupers are not contented.'

'Of course not. When would they be, Mr Bumble?'

'That's the way with these people, ma'am; give 'em a apron full of coals to-day, and they'll come back for another, the day after to-morrow, as brazen as alabaster. Mrs Corney, the great principle of out-of-door relief is, to give the paupers exactly what they don't want; and then they get tired of coming.'

'Dear me! Well, that is a good one, too!'

Mr Bumble took up his hat and stick, as if to go.

'You'll have a very cold walk, Mr Bumble.'

'It blows, ma'am, enough to cut one's ears off.'

The matron looked from the little kettle, to the beadle, who was moving towards the door; and as the beadle coughed, preparatory to bidding her good-night, bashfully inquired whether – whether he wouldn't take a cup of tea?

Mr Bumble instantaneously turned back his collar again; laid his hat and stick upon a chair; and drew another chair up to the table. As he slowly seated himself, he looked at the lady. Mrs Corney applied herself to the task of making his tea.

'Sweet, Mr Bumble?'

'Very sweet, indeed, ma'am.'

He fixed his eyes on Mrs Corney as he said this; and if ever a beadle looked tender, Mr Bumble was that beadle at that moment.

'You have a cat, ma'am, I see and kittens too, I declare.'

'I am so fond of them, Mr Bumble, you can't think. They're so happy, so frolicsome, and so cheerful, that they are quite companions for me.'

'Very nice animals, ma'am, so very domestic.'

'Oh, yes! And so fond of their home too, that it's quite a pleasure, I'm sure.'

'Mrs Corney, ma'am, I mean to say this, ma'am, that any cat, or kitten that could live with you, ma'am, and not be fond of its home, must be an ass, ma'am.'

'Oh, Mr Bumble!'

'It's of no use disguising facts, ma'am,' said Mr Bumble, slowly flourishing the teaspoon with a kind of amorous dignity which made him doubly impressive; 'I would drown it myself with pleasure.'

'Then you're a cruel man and a very hard-hearted man besides.'

'Hard-hearted, ma'am? Hard?'

Mr Bumble resigned his cup without another word; squeezed Mrs Corney's little finger as she took it; and inflicting two open-handed slaps upon his laced waistcoat, gave a mighty sigh, and hitched his chair a very little morsel farther from the fire.

It was a round table; consequently Mr Bumble, moving his chair by little and little, soon began to diminish the distance between himself and the matron; and, continuing to travel round the outer edge of the circle, brought his chair, in time, close to that in which the matron was seated. Indeed, the two chairs touched; and when they did so, Mr Bumble stopped.

Now, if the matron had moved her chair to the right, she would have been scorched by the fire; and if to the left, she must have fallen into Mr Bumble's arms; so being a discreet matron, and no doubt foreseeing these consequences at a glance she remained where she was, and handed Mr Bumble another cup of tea.

'Hard-hearted, Mrs Corney? Are you hard-hearted, Mrs Corney?'

'Dear me! What a very curious question from a single man. What can you want to know for, Mr Bumble?'

The beadle drank his tea to the last drop; finished a piece of toast; whisked the crumbs off his knees; wiped his lips; and deliberately kissed the matron.

'Mr Bumble; Mr Bumble – I shall scream! I am a foolish, excitable, weak creetur.'

'Not weak, ma'am. Are you a weak creetur, Mrs Corney?'

'We are all weak creeturs, Mr Bumble.'

'So we are.'

Nothing was said, on either side, for a minute or two afterwards.

'This is a very comfortable room, ma'am. Another room, and this, ma'am, would be a complete thing.'

'It would be too much for one.'

'But not for two, ma'am. Eh, Mrs Corney? The Board allows you coals, don't they Mrs Corney?'

'And candles.'

'Coals, candles, and a house rent-free. Oh, Mrs Corney, what an angel you are!'

The lady was not proof against this burst of feeling. She sank into Mr Bumble's arms. And that gentleman in his agitation imprinted a passionate kiss upon her chaste nose.

'Such parochial perfection! You know that Mr Slout is worse to-night, my fascinator?'

'Yes.'

'He is the master of this establishment; his death will cause a wacancy; that wacancy must be filled up.'

'Oh Mrs Corney, what a prospect this opens! What a opportunity for a jining of hearts and housekeepings! The little word? The one little, little, little word, my blessed Corney?'

'Ye–yes–yes!'

I love doing that – sexual greed and economic greed in the same scene.

Dickens' most successful females always teetered on the edge of monstrosity. It's with his grotesques, with the women that he didn't want to take to bed, that he erupts into life. He reserved a ferocious scorn, not only for social pretence, but also for the woman beyond sexuality who still yearned for it, like Mrs Skewton, from *Dombey and Son*, who was definitely 'mutton dressed as lamb'.

Mrs Skewton: *Dombey and Son*, 1846–48

Major Bagstock and Mr Dombey beheld advancing towards them, a wheeled chair, in which a lady was seated, indolently steering her carriage by a kind of rudder in front, while it was propelled by some unseen power in the rear. Although the lady was not young, she was very blooming in the face – quite rosy – and her dress and attitude were perfectly juvenile.

'Major Bagstock,' drawled the lady in the chair. 'You false creature! Where do you come from? I can't bear you. You perfidious goblin, how long have you been here, bad man? And can you be a day, or even a minute in the garden of what's-its-name – I never can remember those frightful names – without having your whole Soul and Being inspired by the sight of Nature?

'Mr Dombey is devoted to Nature I trust. I assure you Mr

Mrs Skewton – Phiz

Dombey, Nature intended me for an Aracadian. I am thrown away in society. Cows are my passion. What I have ever sighed for, has been to retreat to a Swiss farm, and live entirely surrounded by cows – and china.

'What I want is heart. What I want, is frankness, confidence, less conventionality, and freer play of soul. We are so dreadfully artificial.'

We were indeed.

Later in the novel, Dickens punishes Mrs Skewton.

Flowers, the Maid, appeared with a pale face to Edith Dombey, saying: 'If you please, Ma'am, I beg your pardon, but can't do nothing with Missis! She's making faces.'

Edith hurried with her to her mother's room.

Cleopatra was arrayed in full dress, with the diamonds, short-sleeves, rouge, curls, teeth, and other juvenility all complete, but Paralysis was not to be deceived, had known her for the object of its errand, and had struck her at her glass, where she lay like a horrible doll that had tumbled down.

One of the most terrifying fates which could befall a respectable Victorian woman was to remain unmarried – to be a spinster. Dickens certainly thought so; his description of Rosa Dartle: 'I concluded in my own mind that she was about thirty years of age, and wished to be married. She was a little dilapidated – like a house – with having been so long to let...'

And Miss Knag, who 'still aimed at youth, though she had shot beyond it years ago'.

And Miss Lucretia Tox: 'a long lean figure, wearing such a faded air that she seemed not to have been made in what linen drapers call "fast colours" originally, and to have little by little washed out'.

Miss Tox had great experience in Hackney cabs, and her starting in one was generally a work of time as she was systematic in the preparatory arrangements.

'Have the goodness, if you please Towlinson,' said Miss Tox, 'first of all to carry out a pen and ink and take his number legibly.'

'Yes, miss,' said Towlinson.

'I'll trouble you also, if you please Towlinson,' said Miss Tox, 'with this card and this shilling. He's to drive to the card and is to understand that he will not on any account have more than the shilling.'

'No, miss,' said Towlinson.

'And – I am sorry to give you so much trouble, Towlinson,' said Miss Tox, looking at him pensively.

'Not at all, Miss,' said Towlinson.

'Mention to the man, then, if you please Towlinson,' said Miss Tox, 'that the Lady's uncle is a magistrate and that if he gives her any of his impertinence he will be punished terribly. You can pretend to say that, if you please Towlinson, in a friendly way and because you know it was done to another man, who died.'

As you probably know, Dickens' works were first published in serial form, in monthly instalments, and in one episode of *David Copperfield*, he introduced an extraordinary character.

Her name is Miss Mowcher and she's a dwarf manicurist and hairdresser. She's based on a real, diminutive chiropodist called Mrs Seymour-Hill, whom Dickens had met when she'd attended his wife, Catherine.

Miss Mowcher: *David Copperfield*, 1849–50

I looked at the doorway and saw nothing. I was still looking at the doorway, thinking that Miss Mowcher was a long while making her appearance, when, to my infinite astonishment, there came waddling round a sofa which stood between me and it, a pursy

Miss Mowcher – Sol Eytinge, 1867

dwarf, of about forty or forty-five, with a very large head and face, and a pair of roguish grey eyes.

'What! My flower! You're there are you! Oh, you naughty boy, fie for shame, what do you do so far away from home? Up to mischief I'll be bound. Oh, you're a downy fellow, Steerforth, so you are, and I'm another ain't I? Ha, ha, ha!

'You'd have betted a hundred pound to five, now, that you wouldn't have seen me here, wouldn't you? Bless you, man alive, I'm everywhere.

'I'm here and there, and where not, like the conjurer's half-crown in the lady's handkercher. Talking of handkerchers – and talking of ladies – what a comfort you are to your blessed mother, ain't you, my dear boy, over one of my shoulders, and I don't say which!

'Oh my stars and what's-their-names! I'm of too full a habit, that's the fact, Steerforth. After a flight of stairs, it gives me as much trouble to draw every breath I want, as if it was a bucket of water.

'If you saw me looking out of an upper window, you'd think I was a fine woman, wouldn't you?

'Happy to make your acquaintance, Mr Copperfield, I'm sure. Face like a peach! Quite tempting! I'm very fond of peaches.

'What a world of gammon and spinnage it is, though, ain't it!

'Look here! Scraps of the Russian Prince's nails. I keep his nails in order for him. Twice a week! Fingers and toes. The Prince's nails do more for me in private families of the genteel sort, than all my talents put together.

'I always carry 'em about. They're the best introduction. If Miss Mowcher cuts the Prince's nails, she must be alright. I give 'em away to the young ladies. They put 'em in albums, I believe.

'Well, well! this is not business. Come, Steerforth, let's explore the polar regions, and have it over.

'If either of you saw my ankles say so, and I'll go home and destroy myself. Well then, I'll consent to live. Now ducky, ducky, ducky, come to Mrs Bond and be killed.

'If Mr Copperfield will take the chair I'll operate on him. And dirt cheap, my chicken. Ain't I volatile, Mr Copperfield?

'Now, I know I'm going to break your hearts, but I am forced to leave you. You must call up all your fortitude, and try to bear it. Good-bye, Mr Copperfield! Take care of yourself, Jockey of Norfolk!

'"Bob swore!" – as the Englishman said for "Good night", when he first learned French, and thought it so like English. "Bob swore", my ducks! Ain't I volatile?'

When the original Miss Mowcher (Mrs Seymour-Hill) read that episode of *David Copperfield* she was mortified. She wrote angrily to Dickens: 'all know you have drawn my portrait – I admit it but the vulgar slang of language I deny.'

Dickens had not meant to hurt her and for once his compassion overcame his genius. He wrote to her lawyer apologising and offered 'to alter the whole design of the character'. He did – and the next time Miss Mowcher appears in the novel, she's a completely different character – utterly saintly and very boring – so I shan't do her!

A woman's portrait – startling in its modernity – is the lesbian, Miss Wade, from *Little Dorrit* – making no apologies for anything.

Miss Wade: The History of a Self-Tormentor, *Little Dorrit*, 1855–57

'I have the misfortune of not being a fool. From a very early age I have detected what those about me thought they hid from me. My childhood was passed with a grandmother; that is to say, with a lady who represented that relative to me, and who took that title on herself; she had no claim to it.

'She had some children of her own family in the house, and some children of other people. All girls; ten in number including me. We all lived together and were educated together. I must

Miss Wade – Sol Eytinge, 1867

have been about twelve years old when I began to see how determinedly those girls patronised me.

'One of them was my chosen friend. I loved that stupid mite in a passionate way that she could no more deserve than I can remember without feeling ashamed of, though I was but a child.

'She had what they called an amiable temper, an affectionate temper. She could distribute, and did distribute, pretty looks and smiles to every one among them. I believe there was not a soul in the place, except myself, who knew that she did it purposely to wound and gall me! Nevertheless, I so loved that unworthy girl that my life was made stormy by my fondness for her. I loved her faithfully; and one time I went home with her for the holidays.

'She was worse at home than she had been at school. She had a crowd of cousins and acquaintances, and we had dances at her house, and went out to dances at other houses, and both at home and out, she tormented my love beyond endurance.

'Her plan was to make them fond of her – and so drive me wild with jealousy.

'When we were left alone in our bedroom at night I would reproach her with my perfect knowledge of her baseness; and then she would cry and cry and say I was cruel, and then I would hold her in my arms 'til morning: loving her as much as ever, and often feeling as if, rather than suffer so, I could so hold her in my arms and plunge to the bottom of a river – where I would still hold her after we both were dead.'

You see, he is such an extraordinary writer: he can create a woman like that with such power and truth and understanding I think, and yet, at the same time be such a male chauvinist that if he hadn't made us laugh so much when we were researching this, he'd have made us very angry.

This, for example, is his perfect wife – Mrs Chirrup from *Sketches for Young Couples*.

[*Music.*]

Mrs Chirrup, *Sketches for Young Couples*, 1840

Mrs Chirrup is the prettiest of all little women and has the prettiest little figure conceivable. She has the neatest little foot, and the softest little voice, and the pleasantest little smile, and the tidiest little curls, and the brightest little eyes, and the quietest little manner, and is, in short, altogether one of the most engaging of all little women, dead or alive.

She is a condensation of all the domestic virtues – a pocket edition of the Young Man's Best Companion – a little woman at a very high pressure, with an amazing quantity of goodness and usefulness in an exceedingly small space.

But if there be one branch of house-keeping in which she excels... it is in the important one – of carving!

Charles Dickens married Catherine Hogarth in 1836 and the most extraordinary thing about the marriage was its ending.

A friend of theirs, Henry Morley, described her:

> Dickens has evidently made a comfortable choice. Mrs Dickens is stout, with a round, very round, rather pretty, very pleasant face, and ringlets on either side of it. One sees in five minutes that she loves her husband and her children and has a warm heart for anyone who won't be satirical, but meet her on her own good-natured footing.

Anyone who won't be satirical!

Well, the years went by, and the children kept coming – twelve births in sixteen years. Catherine grew older and stouter and clumsier. Dickens wrote in 1842, 'Catherine is as near being a donkey as one of her sex can be.'

And Harriet Martineau, a noted feminist of the time, who

60

came to stay with them, wrote: 'Dickens has terrified and depressed her into a dull condition and she never was very clever.'

Now one of Dickens' abiding enthusiasms was the theatre. If he hadn't had a cold on the morning of his audition at Drury Lane Theatre, he would have become a professional actor and throughout his life he adored putting on plays and acting in them.

In 1856 he produced, directed, and starred in a melodrama called *The Frozen Deep*, written by his friend, Wilkie Collins. His two daughters played the female leads. But the following year when the production was re-staged in Manchester, he decided to use professional actresses instead.

He was introduced to and engaged two sisters – Maria Ternan, and her younger sister, Ellen.

Ellen was a young, slender, beautiful, little thing – Dickens fell madly in love with her. He was forty-five years old. She was… seventeen.

[*Music.*]

He bought Ellen a bracelet as a present. It was delivered by mistake to his wife, Catherine. One day their daughter, Kate, came into Mrs Dickens' bedroom and found her mother tying on her bonnet, with the tears pouring down her face…

'Your father insists that I call on Ellen Ternan.'

Kate said, 'You shall not go' – but she did.

You see, Dickens' most passionate enduring relationship was with his public, and he was terrified of losing their affection.

He was determined to devise an acceptable separation. He suggested to Catherine that she should go and live in their country house – Gadshill – while he remained in London, and she should only come to London when he went to the country. Catherine refused.

Then he suggested she should live in France while he remained in England. Catherine refused.

Finally – and most bizarre of all – he suggested that Catherine should live in the upstairs rooms of their house in Tavistock Street, and only come downstairs when they were entertaining visitors.

He got rid of Catherine, but he kept on her sister, Georgina (Mary's replacement), who'd come to live with them when she was fifteen and she never left. She stayed on in Dickens' house, looking after him and her sister's children till the day he died – in fact, he died in Georgina's arms, and she is the principal beneficiary in his will.

I don't think they were ever lovers, but he described her, just as he had described her sister, Mary, as 'the best and truest friend man ever had'. Dickens had a strange affinity with his sisters-in-law.

Further to retain that precious affection of his public... Dickens published a letter on the front page of his own magazine *Household Words*, in *The Morning Post*, in *The Times*, and later in *The New York Tribune*, a letter to the public, in which he said that Catherine and he had 'lived unhappily together for many years', that she had been a bad mother and had lost the affections of her children and that she was of unsound mind. Catherine never responded to these calumnies.

He wanted to publish the letter also in *Punch*, the foremost comic magazine of the day, but the editor, his great friend Mark Lemon, refused because he didn't think it was very funny. Dickens didn't speak to him again for twelve years.

Finally a separation settlement was drawn up. Dickens gave Catherine £600 a year, her own house, Number 70, Gloucester Crescent, her own carriage, and one of her nine children – the eldest son, Charlie – chose to live with his mother. At the time that they left, her youngest child, Edward – known as 'Plorn' – was only six years old.

So the carriage bearing Catherine rolled away for her long stay in Gloucester Crescent. She lived there for twenty-two years. She never saw Dickens again. She only saw her two daughters when they would come for their music lessons to the house opposite.

Catherine would stand at the upstairs window, looking through the lace curtains, waiting for her daughters to turn and wave at her as they went inside. But they never did.

They were reconciled only after Charles Dickens' death and Kate was with her mother when Catherine was dying: Catherine handed her daughter a bundle of letters tied up in blue ribbon – they were Dickens' first letters to her. She said: 'give these to the British Museum, that the world may know he loved me once'.

Catherine is buried in Highgate Cemetery next to her baby daughter Dora. The letters are in the British Museum. Ellen Ternan married a clergyman and lived on 'til 1914. By an extraordinary coincidence she is buried in Southsea, in the same graveyard as Dickens' first love, Maria Beadnell – only Maria lies in an unmarked, pauper's grave.

At the time of the separation, Dickens was writing *Little Dorrit*.

'So, the Bride had mounted into her hansom chariot… and after rolling for a few minutes smoothly over a fair pavement, had begun to jolt through a Slough of Despond, and through a long, long avenue of wrack and ruin.'

Other nuptial carriages are said to have gone the same road, before and since

[*Music under – 'Autumn Leaves'.*]

Miss Havisham: *Great Expectations*, 1860–61

In an armchair, with an elbow resting on the table and her head leaning on that hand, sat the strangest lady I have ever seen, or shall ever see.

She was dressed in rich materials – satins, and lace, and silks – all of white. Her shoes were white. And she had a long white veil, and bridal flowers in her hair, but her hair was white.

She had not quite finished dressing, for she had but one shoe on; the other was on the table near her hand.

I saw that everything within my view which ought to be white, had been white long ago, and had lost its lustre, and was faded and yellow. I saw that the dress had been put upon the rounded figure of a young woman, and that the figure upon which it now hung loose had shrunk to skin and bone.

'Who is it?'

'Pip, ma'am.'

'Pip?'

'Mr Pumblechook's boy, ma'am. Come to play.'

'Come nearer; let me look at you. Come close.'

When I stood before her avoiding her eyes I took note of the surrounding objects in detail. I saw that her watch had stopped at twenty minutes to nine, and that a clock in the room had stopped at twenty minutes to nine.

'Look at me. You are not afraid of a woman who has never seen the sun since you were born? Do you know what I touch here?'

'Yes, ma'am.'

'What do I touch?'

'Your heart.'

'Broken! I am tired, I want diversion, and I have done with men and women. I sometimes have sick fancies and I have a sick fancy that I want to see some play. There, there! play, play, play! You can do that. Call Estella. At the door.'

To stand in the dark in a mysterious passage of an unknown house, bawling Estella to a young lady neither visible nor responsive, and feeling it a dreadful liberty so as to roar out her name, was almost as bad as playing to order.

Miss Havisham and Estella – Sol Eytinge

Estella answered at last, and her light came along the dark passage like a star.

Miss Havisham beckoned her to come close, and took up a jewel from the table, and tried its effect upon her fair young bosom and against her pretty brown hair.

'Let me see you play cards with this boy.'

'With this boy! Why, he is a common labouring-boy!'

'Well? You can break his heart.'

'What do you play, boy?'

'Nothing but Beggar my Neighbour, miss.'

'Beggar him,' said Miss Havisham to Estella. So we sat down to cards. I played the game to an end with Estella, and she beggared me.

[*Music.*]

Many years later I tapped in my old way at the door of Miss Havisham's room. 'Pip's rap,' I heard her say, immediately; 'Come in, Pip.'

She was in her chair near the old table, in the old dress. Sitting near her, with the white shoe, that had never been worn, in her hand, and her head bent as she looked at it, was an elegant lady whom I had never seen.

The lady whom I had never seen before lifted up her eyes and looked archly at me, and then I saw that the eyes were Estella's eyes. But she was so much changed, was so much more beautiful, so much more womanly, that I fancied, as I looked at her, that I slipped hopelessly back into the coarse and common boy again.

'Do you find her much changed, Pip? She was proud and insulting, and you wanted to go away from her. Don't you remember?'

Estella laughed and looked at the shoe in her hand, and laughed again, and looked at me, and put the shoe down. She treated me as a boy still, but she lured me on.

[*Music.*]

Then, Estella being gone and we two left alone, Miss Havisham turned to me and said in a whisper: 'Is she beautiful, graceful, well-grown? Do you admire her? Love her, love her, love her! If she favours you, love her. If she wounds you, love her. If she tears your heart to pieces – and as it gets older and stronger it will tear deeper – love her, love her, love her!'

'Hear me, Pip. I adopted her to be loved. I bred her and educated her, to be loved. I developed her into what she is, that she might be loved. Love her!'

'I'll tell you what real love is. It is blind devotion, unquestioning self-humiliation, utter submission, trust and belief against your-self and against the whole world, giving up your whole heart and soul to the smiter – as I did!'

[*Music under – 'Autumn Leaves' reprise.*]

Some people say that 'Estella' was Ellen Ternan. I think Miss Havisham was Dickens himself.

He died in 1870. He described himself to his great friend John Forster as 'a misplaced and mis-married man, always, as it were, playing hide-and-seek with the world and never finding what Fortune seems to have hidden when he was born'.

I would like to leave you with his tenderest portrait – Miss Flite from *Bleak House*. Miss Flite is a crazy little old lady who, every single day, attends the High Court of Chancery, awaiting a judge-ment on her inheritance, a judgement that may never come…

Miss Flite: *Bleak House*, 1852–53

'I have lived here many years. I pass my days in court; my evenings and my nights here. I find the nights long, for I sleep but little, and think much. That is, of course, unavoidable; being in Chancery.

Miss Flite – Phiz

'I am sorry I cannot offer chocolate. I expect a judgement shortly, and shall then place my establishment on a superior footing.

'At present, I don't mind confessing (in strict confidence), that I sometimes find it difficult to keep up a genteel appearance. I have felt the cold here. I have felt something sharper than cold. It matters very little. Pray excuse the introduction of such mean topics.

'Ah, my birds. I began to keep the little creatures with an object that you will readily comprehend. With the intention of restoring them to liberty. When my judgement should be given. Ye-es! They die in prison, though.

'Their lives, poor silly things, are so short in comparison with Chancery proceedings, that, one by one, the whole collection has died over and over again.

'But I expect a judgement. Shortly. My father expected a judgement. My brother. My sister. They all expected a judgement. The same that I expect. Ye—es. Dead of course.

'I must tell you a secret. I have added to my collection of birds. Two more. I call them the Wards in Jarndyce. They are caged up with all the others.

'With Hope, Joy, Youth, Peace, Rest, Life, Dust, Ashes, Waste, Want, Ruin, Despair, Madness, Death, Cunning, Folly, Words, Wigs, Rags, Sheepskin, Plunder, Precedent, Jargon, Gammon and Spinach!'

The End

George Edmunds' Song by Charles Dickens ('Autumn Leaves')

Autumn leaves, autumn leaves, lie strewn around me here;
Autumn leaves, autumn leaves, how sad, how cold, how drear!
How like the hopes of childhood's day,
Thick clust'ring on the bough!
How like those hopes in their decay—
How faded are they now!
Autumn leaves, autumn leaves, lie strewn around me here;
Autumn leaves, autumn leaves, how sad, how cold, how drear!

Wither'd leaves, wither'd leaves, that fly before the gale:
Withered leaves, withered leaves, ye tell a mournful tale,
Of love once true, and friends once kind,
And happy moments fled:
Dispersed by every breath of wind,
Forgotten, changed, or dead!
Autumn leaves, autumn leaves, lie strewn around me here!
Autumn leaves, autumn leaves, how sad, how cold, how drear!

The Women in the Boxes

Betsey Trotwood

My aunt was a tall, hard-featured lady but by no means ill-looking. There was an inflexibility in her face, in her voice, in her gait and carriage amply sufficient to account for the effect she had made upon a gentle creature like my mother; but her features were rather handsome than otherwise, though unbending and austere. I particularly noticed that she had a quick, bright eye. Her hair, which was grey, was arranged in two plain divisions, under what I believed would be called a mob-cap; I mean a cap much more common then than now, with side pieces fastening under the chin. Her dress was of a lavender colour, and perfectly neat, but scantily made, as if she desired to be as little encumbered as possible. I remember that I thought it, in form, more like a riding-habit, with the superfluous skirt cut off, than anything else. She wore, at her side, a gentle-man's gold watch, if I might judge from its size and make, with an appropriate chain and seals; she had some linen at her throat not unlike a shirt-collar, and things at her wrists like little shirt-wristbands.

Dickens' Women has travelled widely, and played many venues across the world. It was seen in thirteen different places in India. In Visakhapatnam, during a Question and Answer session after the show, a tall, elegant gentleman rose to his feet, smacked his forehead, and demanded to know in an anguished voice, and with great vehemence, 'Where, oh where is Betsey Trotwood?' Where indeed? The truth is that Betsey, along with many other much-admired female characters, was stowed away, in a room in Clapham, in a series of cardboard boxes, containing material that had been read, relished, and then sadly discarded, because there wasn't room for her in the evolving script.

Dickens' friend, and biographer, John Forster called Betsey 'a gnarled and knotted piece of female timber sound to the core'.

It is believed that she was based on Miss Mary Pearson Strong, who lived at Broadstairs, Kent, and who died on 14 January 1855; her former home used to house a Dickens Museum.

Aunt Betsey Trotwood appears early in the novel which Dickens considered to be his best work, *David Copperfield*. She arrives at the home of her dead brother's pretty, gentle, young widow. The sad young woman is heavily pregnant with the eponymous hero, David.

> My father often hinted that she seldom conducted herself like any ordinary Christian; and now, instead of ringing the bell, she came and looked in at the identical window, pressing the end of her nose to that extent, that my poor dear mother used to say that it became flat and white in an instant.
>
> She gave my mother such a turn, that I have always been convinced that I am indebted to Miss Betsey for having been born on a Friday.

It has been said of Dickens that he had to make his characters humorous before he could make them real. This is certainly true of Betsey. Initially, even her tragic history is told with a lightness of touch.

> Miss Trotwood, or Miss Betsey, as my poor mother always called her, when she sufficiently overcame her dread of this formidable personage to mention her at all (which was seldom), had been married to a husband younger than herself, who was very handsome, except in the sense of the homely adage, 'handsome is, as handsome does,' – for he

was strongly suspected of having beaten Miss Betsey and even once, on a disputed question of supplies, made some hasty but determined arrangements to throw her out of a two pair of stairs' window.

Determined that the soon-to-be-delivered baby is to be a girl named Betsey Trotwood Copperfield, the formidable aunt terrorises the amiable doctor Mr Chillip (another glorious Dickens name):

> 'The baby,' said my aunt, 'How is she?'
>
> 'Ma'am,' returned Mr Chillip 'I apprehended you had known. It's a boy.'
>
> My aunt never said a word, but took her bonnet by the strings, in the manner of a sling, aimed a blow at Mr Chillip's head with it, put it on bent, and walked out and never came back.

She does return later in the book. After his young mother's death in childbirth, David is sent by his unfeeling stepfather to work in a warehouse. Just as in the blacking factory of Dickens' own childhood, the unfortunate workforce wash and label wine bottles. Dickens dips his pen in his own heart's blood and, as David, writes:

> I know enough of the world now, to have almost lost the capacity of being much surprised by anything; but it is a matter of some surprise to me even now, that I can have been so easily thrown away at such an age. A child of excellent abilities, and with strong powers of observation, quick, eager, delicate, and soon hurt bodily or mentally, it seems wonderful to me that nobody should have made a sign on my behalf. But none was made; and I became at ten years old, a little labouring hind in the service of Murdstone and Grinsby.

When David runs away from Murdstone and Grinsby he makes his way to Dover, to Aunt Betsey Trotwood.

> Again and again, and a hundred times again, since the night when the thought first occurred to me and banished sleep, I had gone over that old story of my poor mother's about my birth, which it had been one of my great delights in the old time, to hear tell, and which I knew by heart. My aunt walked into that story, and walked out of it, a dread and awful personage; but there was one little trait in her behaviour which I liked to dwell on, and which gave me some faint shadow of encouragement. I could not forget how my mother had thought that she felt her touch her pretty hair with no ungentle hand; and though it might have been altogether my mother's fancy, and might have had no foundation whatever, in fact, I made a little picture out of it, of my terrible aunt relenting towards the girlish beauty that I recollected so well and loved so much, which softened the whole narrative. It is very possible that it had been in my mind a long while, and had gradually engendered my determination.

Rescued from the function of being the 'terrible aunt', Betsey becomes that rarity among Dickens' women, a mature woman who is sensible, kind, wise and genuinely good. She is neither satirised, nor idealised. She is shown to be tactfully helpful to all; to Mr Dick, whom she cares for having saved him from the asylum into which his brother had cast him; and to David, for whom she defies the evil Murdstones and whom she clothes, houses, loves and, most glorious of all, sends to school. She does, however, rename him Trotwood (shortened to Trot), an echo of the female child he failed to be. She is instrumental in saving the Micawbers, and Little Em'ly. Well, she succeeds in sending them to Australia, which was meant to equal salvation.

One yearns to know more about Miss Mary Pearson Strong and her influence on Dickens. Dickens' son, Charles, recalled how Miss Strong fiercely defended her property from donkeys, which inspired the brilliant set piece:

> 'I won't be trespassed upon, I won't allow it. Go away! Janet, turn him round. Lead him off!' and I saw from behind my aunt, a sort of hurried battle-piece, in which the donkey stood, resisting everybody, with all his four legs planted different ways, while Janet tried to lead him round by the bridle, Mr Murdstone tried to lead him on, Miss Murdstone struck at Janet with her parasol, and several boys who had come to see the engagement, shouted vigorously. But my aunt suddenly descrying among them the young malefactor who was the donkey's guardian, and who was one of the most inveterate offenders against her, though hardly in his teens, rushed out to the scene of action, pounced upon him, captured him, dragged him, with his jacket over his head, and his heels grinding into the ground into the garden, and, calling upon Janet to fetch the constables and justices, that he might be taken, tried, and executed on the spot, held him at bay there. This part of the business, however, did not last long; for the young rascal, being expert at a variety of feints and dodges, of which my aunt has no conception, soon went whooping away, leaving some deep impression of his nailed boots in the flower-beds, and taking his donkey in triumph with him.

If one were to disagree with Kate that her father 'didn't really understand women', it would be in contemplation of Betsey and her continuing love for her cruel husband. She is not corroded by her love, as is Miss Havisham. The errant husband is a recurring, mysterious presence in the novel. Betsey confides in the young David:

'Betsey Trotwood don't look a likely subject for the tender passion,' said my aunt, composedly, 'but the time was, Trot, when she believed in that man most entirely. When she loved him, Trot, right well. When there was no proof of attachment and affection that she would not have given him. He repaid her by breaking her fortune, and nearly breaking her heart. So she put all that sentiment in a grave, and filled it up, and flattened it down.'

'My dear, good Aunt!'

'I left him,' my aunt proceeded laying her hand as usual on the back of mine, 'generously. I may say at this distance of time, Trot, that I left him, generously. He had been so cruel to me, that I might have effected a separation on easy terms for myself; but I did not. He soon made ducks and drakes of what I gave him, sank lower and lower, married another woman. I believe, became an adventurer, a gambler, and a cheat. What he is now you see. But he was a fine looking man when I married him,' said my aunt, with an echo of her old pride and admiration in her tone, 'and I believed him – I was a fool! – to be the soul of honour!

'... I give him more money than I can afford, at intervals, when he reappears, to go away. I was a fool when I married him; and I am so far an incurable fool on that subject, that, for the sake of what I once believed him to be, I wouldn't have this shadow of my idle fancy hardly dealt with. For I was in earnest, Trot, if ever a woman was.'

My aunt dismissed the matter, with a heavy sigh, and smoothed her dress.

'There my dear,' she said. 'Now you know the beginning, middle, and end, and all about it. We won't mention the subject to one another any more; neither, of course, will you mention it to anybody else. This is my grumpy, frumpy story and we'll keep it to ourselves, Trot.'

Philanthropic Ladies

In *The Miracle of Christmas*, a collection of Christmas stories by Charles Dickens and others, there is a story of strange sentimentality by Mrs Harriet Beecher Stowe, the American writer, and authoress of *Uncle Tom's Cabin*. It is called 'Christmas in Poganuc' and features a blonde, blue-eyed little girl, of nauseating cuteness, called Dolly. Dolly features prominently in 'People of Poganuc', Mrs Beecher Stowe's semi-autobiographical collection of stories which was published in 1878.

Uncle Tom's Cabin was published serially across America from 1850 to 1852. Dickens may have been less than enthusiastic about Mrs Stowe's talents as a writer, but he ardently praised her virtues as a campaigner, and in an article in *Household Words*, written jointly with Morley, he declared *Uncle Tom's Cabin* to be 'a noble work; full of high power, lofty humanity'. Then he dipped his pen in its most brilliant, satirical ink, and with all the power of his wicked genius he created Mrs Jellyby, the anti-slavery campaigner in *Bleak House* (published 1853).

> 'Mrs Jellyby,' said Mr Kenge, standing with his back to the fire, and casting his eyes over the dusty hearth rug as if it were Mrs Jellyby's biography, 'is a lady of very remarkable strength of character, who devotes herself entirely to the public. She has devoted herself to an excessive variety of public subjects, at various times, and is at present (until something else attracts her) devoted to the subject of Africa; with a view to the general cultivation of the coffee berry – and the natives – and the happy settlement on the banks of the African rivers, of our superabundant home population.'

Mrs Jellyby is introduced in Chapter Four of *Bleak House*, headed 'Telescopic Philanthropy'. When Esther, Amy and Richard arrive at Mrs Jellyby's house,

There was a confused little crowd of people, principally children, gathered about the house at which we stopped, which had a tarnished brass plate upon the door, with the inscription, JELLYBY.

'Don't be frightened!' said Mr Guppy, looking in at the coach window, 'One of the young Jellybys gone and got his head through the area railings.'

Numerous other little Jellybys, dirty and neglected, tumble down stairs and meet with multitudinous accidents, 'notched on their arms and legs', and are gently ignored by their mother, who is calm and pretty 'with handsome eyes, though they had a curious habit of seeming to look a long way off. As if – I am quoting Richard again – they could see nothing nearer than Africa!'

Mrs Jellyby had very good hair, but was too much occupied with her African duties to brush it. The shawl in which she had been loosely muffled, dropped onto her chair when she advanced to us; and as she turned to resume her seat, we could not help noticing that her dress didn't nearly meet up across the back, and that the open space was railed across with a lattice work of stay-lace – like a summer-house...

'You find me, my dears, as usual very busy; but that you will excuse. The African project at present employs my whole time. It involves me in correspondence with public bodies, and with private individuals anxious for the welfare of their species all over the country. I am happy to say it is advancing. We hope by this time next year to have from a hundred and fifty to two hundred healthy families cultivating coffee and educating the natives of Borrioboola-Gha, on the left bank of the Niger.'

As if she were not joy enough Mrs Jellyby is joined in the story by Mrs Pardiggle. In a brilliant commentary on charity ladies, Dickens gives to Mr Jarndyce the observation that 'there were two classes of charitable people; one, the people who did a little and made a good deal of noise; the other, the people who did a great deal, and made no noise at all.'

Mrs Pardiggle, it is made clear, belongs to the first category.

She was a formidable style of lady, with spectacles, a prominent nose, and a loud voice, who had the effect of wanting a great deal of room. And she really did, for she knocked down little chairs with her skirts that were quite a great way off. As only Ada and I were at home, we received her timidly; for she seemed to come in like cold weather, and so make the little Pardiggles blue as they followed.

'These, young ladies,' said Mrs Pardiggle, 'are my five boys. You may have seen their names in a printed subscription list (perhaps more than one) in the possession of our esteemed friend, Mr Jarndyce. Egbert, my eldest (twelve), is the boy who sent out his pocket money, to the amount of five-and-threepence, to the Tockahoopo Indians, Gerald my second (ten-and-a-half) is the child who contributed two-and-ninepence to The Great Smithers Testimonial. Francis, my third (nine), one-and-sixpence-halfpenny; Felix, my fourth (seven), eightpence to the Superannuated Widows; Alfred, my youngest (five), has voluntarily enrolled himself in the Infant Bonds of Joy, and is pledged never, through life, to use tobacco, in any form.'

We had never seen such dissatisfied children. It was not merely that they were weakened and shrivelled – though they were certainly that too – but they looked absolutely ferocious with discontent. At the mention of the Tockahoopo Indians, I could really have supposed Egbert to be one of the most baleful members of the tribe, he gave me such a savage frown. The face of each child, as the amount of his contribution was mentioned, darkened in a peculiarly vindictive manner, but his was by far the worst. I must except, however, the little recruit into the Infant Bonds of Joy, who was stolidly, and evenly, miserable.

In the final chapter of *Bleak House*, 'The Close of Esther's Narrative', when all loose ends are tied up, and all virtue is rewarded, reference is made to Mrs Jellyby:

> She has been disappointed in Borrioboola-Gha, which turned out a failure, in consequence of the king of Borrioboola wanting to sell everybody who survived the climate, for Rum; but she has taken up with the rights of women to sit in Parliament, and Caddy tells me it is a mission involving more correspondence than the old one.

Even Mrs Pankhurst would forgive a man who compared stay-lacing to a summer-house.

Urania Cottage

'Gaslight Fairies' from *Household Words*

> Nothing is easier than for any one of us to get into a pulpit, or upon a tub, or a stump, or a platform, and blight (so far as with our bilious and complacent breath we can) any class of small people we may choose to select. But, it by no means follows that because it is easy and safe it is right. Even these very gaslight Fairies, now! Why should I be bitter on them because they are shabby personages, tawdrily dressed for the passing hour, and then to be shabby again?
> ... Poor, good humoured, patient, fond of a little self display perhaps (sometimes but far from always), they will come trudging through the mud, leading brother and sister lesser Fairies by the hand, and will hover about in the dark

stage-entrances, shivering and chattering in their shrill way, and earning their little money hard…

Let me […] take a single fairy […] and sketch the Family Picture. I select Miss Fairy, aged three-and-twenty, lodging within cannon range of Waterloo Bridge, London – not alone, but with her mother, Mrs Fairy, disabled by chronic rheumatism, in the knees; and with her father, Mr Fairy, principally employed in lurking about a public-house, and waylaying the theatrical profession for twopence wherewith to purchase a glass of old ale, that he may have something warming on his stomach (which has been cold for fifteen years); and with Miss Rosina Fairy, Miss Angelica Fairy, and Master Edmund Fairy, aged respectively, four-teen, ten and eight. Miss Fairy has an engagement of twelve shillings a week – sole means of preventing the Fairy family from coming to a deadlock. To be sure, at this time of year the three young Fairies have a nightly engagement to come out of a Pumpkin as French soldiers; but, its advantage to the housekeeping is rendered nominal, by that dreadful old Mr Fairy's making it a legal formality to draw the money himself every Saturday – and never coming home until his stomach is warmed, and the money gone…

A hard life this for Miss Fairy, I say, and a dangerous! And it is good to see her, in the midst of it, so watchful of Miss Rosina Fairy, who otherwise might come to harm one day.

Always at his superb best when writing about theatre people, it is Dickens the compassionate philanthropist whom we encounter and admire, in that article from *Household Words*. Here, he is the articulate advocate for the understanding of the plight of the 'small people'.

His philanthropy was intensely personal and it brought into his life one of his most successful relationships with a woman,

Angela Burdett-Coutts (1814–1906). Her life was as vivid as his, though in contrast to the poverty of his childhood, she came from a world of extreme wealth. At the age of twenty-three she inherited a fortune from her grandfather. It was around three million pounds, a vast sum in the currency of the time, and it made her the richest heiress in England. She devoted herself generously and imaginatively to a wide range of charitable ventures. She was instrumental in the establishment of the NSPCC; was President of the ladies' committee of the RSPCA; she established several social housing schemes, including Columbia Market; set up church schools; supported the Arts; and, rather charmingly, was responsible for setting up a scheme to provide drinking fountains for dogs, and was President of the Beekeepers Association (1878–1906). Her private life was colourful. She had a loving relationship with a female companion for fifty-two years; is said to have proposed to the Duke of Wellington; and she outraged Society when, at the age of sixty-six, she married her secretary, the twenty-nine-year-old, magnificently named, William Lehman Ashmead Bartlett. He changed his name to Burdett-Coutts, and became MP for Westminster in 1881.

Together she and Dickens created Urania Cottage, an Asylum for Fallen Women, later to be called A Home.

Dickens tirelessly involved himself organising the daily schedule, interviewing the girls and taking their case histories, appointing staff, dealing with practicalities like blocked drains, overseeing all accounts and answering frequent summons to administer discipline on the premises to erring young women who were drunk and disorderly.

This letter was handed to the fallen women who were chosen as likely candidates for a stay at Urania Cottage:

An extract from Dickens' Appeal to Fallen Women

You will see, on beginning to read this letter that it is not addressed to you by name. But I address it to a woman – a very young woman still – who was born to be happy, and has lived miserably, who has no prospect before her but sorrow, or behind her but a wasted youth who, if she has ever been a mother, has felt shame, instead of pride, in her own unhappy child.

You are such a person or this letter would not be put into your hands. If you have ever wished (I know you must have done so sometimes) for a chance of rising out of your sad life, and having friends, a quiet home, means of being useful to yourself and others, peace of mind, self-respect, everything you have lost, pray read it attentively and reflect upon it afterwards. I am going to offer you not the chance but the certainty of all these blessings, if you will exert yourself to deserve them. And do not think that I write to you as if I felt myself very much above you, or wished to hurt your feelings by reminding you of the situation in which you are placed. GOD forbid! I mean nothing but kindness to you and I write as if you were my sister.

Dickens was rare among those concerned with the 'working girls' of the time. He was compassionate towards them. He believed in their reformation. His home offered the young women kindness, friendship and hope. It is true that his ultimate hope for the dozen or so young women occupying Urania Cottage, at any one time, was that they would emigrate to Australia and marry, and it was for this purpose that they were being trained. They often had difficulty in appreciating the difference between voluntary emigration and transportation. In the story of Martha Endell, the very fallen woman in *David Copperfield*, this fate was the happy ending that Dickens presented to his readers. This romantically satisfactory conclusion may have been more for their pleasure than from any practical understanding that he gained from the lively occupants of Urania Cottage. Mr Peggotty returns from Australia with this story of Martha's happy ending.

> 'Mr Peggotty drew his hand from across his face, and with a half suppressed sigh looked up from the fire.
>
> 'Is Martha with you yet?' I asked.
>
> 'Martha,' he replied, 'got married, Mas'r Davy, in the second year. A young man, a farm-labourer, as come by us on his way to market with his masr's drays – a journey of over five hundred miles theer and back – made offers fur to take her fur his wife (wives is very scarce theer), and then to set up for their two selves in the Bush. She spoke fur me to tell him her trew story. I did. They was married, and they live fower hundred miles away from any voices but their own and the singing birds.'

In his second novel *Oliver Twist*, written eleven years before the opening of Urania Cottage, Dickens writes of Nancy and Bet,

> They wore a great deal of hair, not very neatly turned up behind, and were rather untidy about the shoes and stockings. They were not exactly pretty perhaps; but they had a great deal of colour in their faces, and looked quite stout and healthy. Being remarkably free and easy with their manners, Oliver thought them very nice girls indeed. Which there is no doubt they were.

Dickens saw such women every night, as he walked back from the Marshalsea prison, where he visited his parents after working at the blacking factory, walking through Seven Dials, the most notorious part of London, to his lodgings with Mrs Roylance (Mrs Pipchin) in Little College Street, Camden Town. He was twelve years old, he looked with the eye of a child at the vicious, the violent, the drunken, the desperate. He never forgot what he saw and his gaze at the world continued childlike and unfiltered, until he died.

I can't exactly make a case for Mrs Bardell as based on a real personage in Dickens' life, but her blend of silliness and sexual desperation seems to recur very often in his females. The giggling, the glances, the carefully chosen hints at a forthcoming nuptial are frequent characteristics of his women; from whom such portraits were drawn is never quite clear. I think Dickens just saw women as intrinsically foolish and possibly sexually rapacious, with a few exceptions like Mrs Gaskell, George Eliot and Baroness Burdett-Coutts. Here's one such creature.

'Mrs Bardell,' said Mr Pickwick, at last, as that amiable female approached the termination of a prolonged dusting of the apartment.

'Sir,' said Mrs Bardell.

'Your little boy is a very long time gone.'

'Why it's a good long way to the Borough, sir,' remonstrated Mrs Bardell.

'Ah,' said Mr Pickwick, 'very true; so it is.'

Mr Pickwick relapsed into silence, and Mrs Bardell resumed her dusting.

'Mrs Bardell,' said Mr Pickwick, at the expiration of a few minutes.

'Sir,' said Mrs Bardell again.

'Do you think it a much greater expense to keep two people, than to keep one?'

'La, Mr Pickwick,' said Mrs Bardell, colouring up to the very border of her cap, as she fancied she observed a species of matrimonial twinkle in the eyes of her lodger; 'La, Mr Pickwick, what a question!'

'Well, but do you?' inquired Mr Pickwick.

'That depends,' said Mrs Bardell, approaching the duster

very near to Mr Pickwick's elbow which was planted on the table, 'that depends a good deal upon the person, you know, Mr Pickwick; and whether it's a saving and careful person, sir.

'That's very true,' said Mr Pickwick, 'but the person I have in my eye (here he looked very hard at Mrs Bardell) I think possesses these qualities; and has, moreover, a considerable knowledge of the world, and a great deal of sharpness, Mrs Bardell, which may be of material use to me.'

'La, Mr Pickwick,' said Mrs Bardell, the crimson rising to her cap-border again.

'I do,' said Mr Pickwick, growing energetic, as was his wont in speaking of a subject which interested him – 'I do, indeed; and to tell you the truth, Mrs Bardell, I have made up my mind.'

'Dear me, sir,' exclaimed Mrs Bardell.

'You'll think it very strange now,' said the amiable Mr Pickwick, with a good-humoured glance at his companion, 'that I never consulted you about this matter, and never even mentioned it, till I sent your little boy out this morning – eh?'

Mrs Bardell could only reply by a look. She had long worshipped Mr Pickwick at a distance, but here she was, all at once, raised to a pinnacle to which her wildest and most extravagant hopes had never dared to aspire. Mr Pickwick was going to propose – a deliberate plan, too – sent her little boy to the Borough, to get him out of the way – how thoughtful – how considerate!

'Well,' said Mr Pickwick, 'what do you think?'

'Oh, Mr Pickwick,' said Mrs Bardell, trembling with agitation, 'you're very kind, sir.'

'It'll save you a good deal of trouble, won't it?' said Mr Pickwick.

'Oh, I never thought anything of the trouble, sir,' replied Mrs Bardell; 'and, of course, I should take more trouble to please you then, than ever; but it is so kind of you, Mr Pickwick, to have so much consideration for my loneliness.'

'Ah, to be sure,' said Mr Pickwick; 'I never thought of that. When I am in town, you'll always have somebody to sit with you. To be sure, so you will.'

'I am sure I ought to be a very happy woman,' said Mrs Bardell.

'And your little boy –' said Mr Pickwick.

'Bless his heart!' interposed Mrs Bardell, with a maternal sob.

'He, too, will have a companion,' resumed Mr Pickwick, 'a lively one, who'll teach him, I'll be bound, more tricks in a week than he would ever learn in a year.' And Mr Pickwick smiled placidly.

'Oh, you dear –' said Mrs Bardell.

Mr Pickwick started.

'Oh, you kind, good, playful dear,' said Mrs Bardell; and without more ado, she rose from her chair, and flung her arms round Mr Pickwick's neck, with a cataract of tears and a chorus of sobs.

'Bless my soul,' cried the astonished Mr Pickwick; 'Mrs Bardell, my good woman – dear me, what a situation – pray consider. – Mrs Bardell, don't – if anybody should come –'

'Oh, let them come,' exclaimed Mrs Bardell frantically; 'I'll never leave you – dear, kind, good soul;' and, with these words, Mrs Bardell clung the tighter.

'Mercy upon me,' said Mr Pickwick, struggling violently, 'I hear somebody coming up the stairs. Don't, don't, there's a good creature, don't.'

But entreaty and remonstrance were alike unavailing; for Mrs Bardell had fainted in Mr Pickwick's arms; and before he could gain time to deposit her on a chair, Master Bardell entered the room, ushering in Mr Tupman, Mr Winkle, and Mr Snodgrass.

Mr Pickwick was struck motionless and speechless. He stood with his lovely burden in his arms, gazing vacantly on the countenances of his friends, without the slightest attempt at recognition or explanation. They, in their turn, stared at him; and Master Bardell, in his turn, stared at everybody …

'Now help me, lead this woman downstairs.'

'Oh, I am better now,' said Mrs Bardell faintly.

'Let me lead you downstairs,' said the ever-gallant Mr Tupman.

'Thank you, sir – thank you;' exclaimed Mrs Bardell hysterically.

And downstairs she was led accordingly, accompanied by her affectionate son.

'I cannot conceive,' said Mr Pickwick when his friend returned – 'I cannot conceive what has been the matter with that woman. I had merely announced to her my intention of keeping a man-servant, when she fell into the extraordinary paroxysm in which you found her. Very extraordinary thing.'

The men are, as usual, utterly puzzled by the hysteria they've engendered.

Among the women who have a right to appear in *Dickens' Women* are the actresses whom he affectionately satirises in *Nicholas Nickleby*. As actresses ourselves, we know of no better description of a group of actresses than this one, from *Nicholas Nickleby*.

The ladies were gathered in a little knot by themselves round the rickety table before mentioned. There was Miss Snevellicci – who could do anything, from a medley dance to Lady Macbeth, and also always played some part in blue silk knee-smalls at her benefit – glancing, from the depths of her coal-scuttle straw bonnet, at Nicholas, and affecting to be absorbed in the recital of a diverting story to her friend Miss Ledrook, who had brought her work, and was making up a ruff in the most natural manner possible. There was Miss Belvawney – who seldom aspired to speaking parts, and usually went on as a page in white silk hose, to stand with one leg bent, and contemplate the audience, or to go in and out after Mr Crummles in stately tragedy – twisting up the ringlets of the beautiful Miss Bravassa, who had once had her likeness taken 'in character' by an engraver's apprentice, whereof impressions were hung up for sale in the pastry-cook's window, and the greengrocer's, and at the circulating library, and the box-office, whenever the announce bills came out for her annual night. There was Mrs Lenville, in a very limp bonnet and veil, decidedly in that way in which she would wish to be if she truly loved Mr Lenville; there was Miss Gazingi, with an imitation ermine boa tied in a loose knot round her neck, flogging Mr Crummles, junior, with both ends, in fun. Lastly, there was Mrs Grudden in a brown cloth pelisse and a beaver bonnet, who assisted Mrs Crummles in her domestic affairs, and took money at the doors, and dressed the ladies, and swept the house, and held the prompt book when everybody else was on for the last scene, and acted any kind of part on any emergency without ever learning it, and was put down in the bills under any name or names whatever, that occurred to Mr Crummles as looking well in print.

Mr Folair having obligingly confided these particulars to Nicholas, left him to mingle with his fellows; the work of personal introduction was completed by Mr Vincent Crummles, who publicly heralded the new actor as a prodigy of genius and learning.

'I beg your pardon,' said Miss Snevellicci, sidling towards Nicholas, 'but did you ever play at Canterbury?'

'I never did,' replied Nicholas.

'I recollect meeting a gentleman at Canterbury,' said Miss Snevellicci, 'only for a few moments, for I was leaving the company as he joined it, so like you that I felt almost certain it was the same.'

'I see you now for the first time,' rejoined Nicholas with all due gallantry. 'I am sure I never saw you before; I couldn't have forgotten it.'

'Oh, I'm sure – it's very flattering of you to say so,' retorted Miss Snevellicci with a graceful bend. 'Now I look at you again, I see that the gentleman at Canterbury hadn't the same eyes as you – you'll think me very foolish for taking notice of such things, won't you?'

'Not at all,' said Nicholas. 'How can I feel otherwise than flattered by your notice in any way?'

'Oh! you men are such vain creatures!' cried Miss Snevellicci. Whereupon, she became charmingly confused, and, pulling out her pocket-handkerchief from a faded pink silk reticule with a gilt clasp, called to Miss Ledrook – 'Led, my dear,' said Miss Snevellicci.

'Well, what is the matter?' said Miss Ledrook.

'It's not the same.'

'Not the same what?'

'Canterbury – you know what I mean. Come here! I want to speak to you.'

But Miss Ledrook wouldn't come to Miss Snevellicci, so Miss Snevellicci was obliged to go to Miss Ledrook, which she did, in a skipping manner that was quite fascinating; and Miss Ledrook evidently joked Miss Snevellicci about being struck with Nicholas; for, after some playful whispering, Miss Snevellicci hit Miss Ledrook very hard on the backs of her hands, and retired up, in a state of pleasing confusion.

I cannot resist the Infant Phenomenon, a prominent member of the Vincent Crummles Theatre Company, in Portsmouth.

As Mrs Vincent Crummles recrossed back to the table, there bounded on to the stage from some mysterious inlet, a little girl in a dirty white frock with tucks up to the knees, short trousers, sandaled shoes, white spencer, pink gauze bonnet, green veil and curl papers; who turned a pirouette, cut twice in the air, turned another pirouette, then, looking off at the opposite wing, shrieked, bounded forward to within six inches of the footlights, and fell into a beautiful attitude of terror, as a shabby gentleman in an old pair of buff slippers came in at one powerful slide, and chattering his teeth, fiercely brandished a walking-stick.

'Bravo!' cried Nicholas, resolved to make the best of everything. 'Beautiful!'

'This, sir,' said Mr Vincent Crummles, bringing the maiden forward, 'this is the infant phenomenon – Miss Ninetta Crummles.'

'Your daughter?' inquired Nicholas.

'My daughter – my daughter,' replied Mr Vincent Crummles; 'the idol of every place we go into, sir. We have had complimentary letters about this girl, sir, from the nobility and gentry of almost every town in England.'

'I am not surprised at that,' said Nicholas; 'she must be quite a natural genius.'

'Quite a –!' Mr Crummles stopped: language was not powerful enough to describe the infant phenomenon. 'I'll tell you what, sir,' he said; 'the talent of this child is not to be imagined. She must be seen, sir – seen – to be ever so faintly appreciated. There; go to your mother, my dear.'

'May I ask how old she is?' inquired Nicholas.

'You may, sir,' replied Mr Crummles, looking steadily in his questioner's face, as some men do when they have doubts about being implicitly believed in what they are going to say. 'She is ten years of age, sir.'

'Not more!'

'Not a day.'

'Dear me!' said Nicholas, 'it's extraordinary.'

It was; for the infant phenomenon, though of short stature, had a comparatively aged countenance, and had moreover been precisely the same age – not perhaps to the full extent of the memory of the oldest inhabitant, but certainly for five good years. But she had been kept up late every night, and put upon an unlimited allowance of gin-and-water from infancy, to prevent her growing tall, and perhaps this system of training had produced in the infant phenomenon, these additional phenomena.

Miss Ninetta Crummles is a miniature harridan. But Dickens also specialised in the adult variety and his exploration of the truly evil aspect of the Feminine is fully realised by Madame Defarge in *A Tale of Two Cities*.

Madame Defarge, his wife, sat in the shop behind the counter as he came in. Madame Defarge was a stout woman of about his own age, with a watchful eye that seldom seemed to look at anything, a large hand heavily ringed, a steady face, strong features, and great composure of manner. There was a character about Madame Defarge, from which one might have predicated that she did not often make mistakes against herself in any of the reckonings over which she presided. Madame Defarge being sensitive to cold, was wrapped in fur, and had a quantity of bright shawl twined about her head, though not to the conceal-ment of her large earrings. Her knitting was before her, but she had laid it down to pick her teeth with a toothpick. Thus engaged, with her right elbow supported by her left hand, Madame Defarge said nothing when her lord came in, but coughed just one grain of cough. This, in combina-tion with the lifting of her darkly defined eyebrows over her toothpick by the breadth of a line, suggested to her husband that he would do well to look round the shop among the customers, for any new customer who had dropped in while he stepped over the way.

Madame Defarge slightly waved her hand, to imply that she heard, and might be relied upon to arrive in good time, and so went through the mud, and round the corner of the prison wall. The Vengeance and the Juryman, looking after her as she walked away, were highly appreciative of her fine figure, and her superb moral endowments.

There were many women at that time, upon whom the time laid a dreadfully disfiguring hand; but, there was not one among them more to be dreaded than this ruthless woman, now taking her way along the streets. Of a strong and fearless character, of shrewd sense and readiness, of great determination, of that kind of beauty which not only seems to impart to its possessor firmness and animosity, but to strike into others an instinctive recognition of those qualities; the troubled time would have heaved her up, under any circumstances. But, imbued from her childhood with a brooding sense of wrong, and an inveterate hatred of a class, opportunity had developed her into a tigress. She was absolutely without pity. If she had ever had the virtue in her, it had quite gone out of her.

It was nothing to her, that an innocent man was to die for the sins of his forefathers; she saw, not him, but them. It was nothing to her, that his wife was to be made a widow and his daughter an orphan; that was insufficient punishment, because they were her natural enemies and her prey, and as such had no right to live. To appeal to her, was made hopeless by her having no sense of pity, even for herself. If she had been laid low in the streets, in any of the many encounters in which she had been engaged, she would not have pitied herself; nor, if she had been ordered to the axe to-morrow, would she have gone to it with any softer feeling than a fierce desire to change places with the man who sent her there.

Such a heart Madame Defarge carried under her rough robe. Carelessly worn, it was a becoming robe enough, in a certain weird way, and her dark hair looked rich under her coarse red cap. Lying hidden in her bosom, was a loaded pistol. Lying hidden at her waist, was a sharpened dagger. Thus accoutred, and walking with the confident tread of such a character, and with the supple freedom of a woman who had habitually walked in her girlhood, bare-foot and bare-legged, on the brown sea-sand, Madame Defarge took her way along the streets.

Dickens hasn't created a real woman. It's as if he's dragged from the depths of his own fears an iconic distillation of feminine power, misdirected and distorted.

There is a problem with Charles Dickens, as there is with all geniuses whose lives seem to betray the gifts they own. We want a good writer to be a good man.

But when I read him and most especially when I perform him, I cannot but be delighted, enriched and continually surprised. His humanity transcends his cruelty; the prejudice, the sense of grievance of which he is occasionally guilty seem to fade and, at the end, I am left with the triumph of his imagination and I am happy to settle for that.

Charles Dickens' Bibliography

The Pickwick Papers: Monthly serial, April 1836 to November 1837

The Adventures of Oliver Twist: Monthly serial in *Bentley's Miscellany*, February 1837 to April 1839

The Life and Adventures of Nicholas Nickleby: Monthly serial, April 1838 to October 1839

The Old Curiosity Shop: Weekly serial in *Master Humphrey's Clock*, 25 April 1840 to 6 February 1841

Barnaby Rudge: A Tale of the Riots of 'Eighty': Weekly serial in *Master Humphrey's Clock*, 13 February 1841 to 27 November 1841

A Christmas Carol 1843: The Life and Adventures of Martin Chuzzlewit: Monthly serial, January 1843 to July 1844

The Chimes: 1844

The Cricket on the Hearth: 1845

The Battle of Life: 1846

Dombey and Son: Monthly serial, October 1846 to April 1848

The Haunted Man and the Ghost's Bargain: 1848

David Copperfield: Monthly serial, May 1849 to November 1850

Bleak House: Monthly serial, March 1852 to September 1853

Hard Times: For These Times: Weekly serial in *Household Words*, 1 April 1854 to 12 August 1854

Little Dorrit: Monthly serial, December 1855 to June 1857

A Tale of Two Cities: Weekly serial in *All the Year Round*, 30 April 1859 to 26 November 1859

Great Expectations: Weekly serial in *All the Year Round*, 1 December 1860 to 3 August 1861

Our Mutual Friend: Monthly serial, May 1864 to November 1865

The Mystery of Edwin Drood: Monthly serial, April 1870 to September 1870. Only six of twelve planned numbers completed.

Acknowledgments

With grateful thanks to F.R. Leavis, Q.D. Leavis, Michael Slater, Claire Tomalin and Angus Wilson.

Biographical Note

Sonia Fraser trained as an actress at the Bristol Old Vic Theatre School. As an actress she worked with several major theatre companies, including two years with the Royal Shakespeare Company. She was twice a member of the BBC Radio Drama Rep. and it was when they were both working in Radio that she and Miriam Margolyes first met. Her career as a director began when she ran the Studio Theatre at Colchester Mercury Theatre. She has always been interested in new writing, and has won three Fringe First Awards at the Edinburgh Festival. She has co-written a television series, which is about the contemporary life of an English village, and which is filled with Dickensian characters. (www.soniafraser.co.uk)

Miriam Margolyes was born in Oxford and read English Literature at Newnham College, Cambridge. She joined the BBC Radio Drama Repertory Company in 1965, and since then has worked continuously in theatre, television and films, playing everything from Ranevskaya in *The Cherry Orchard* to Lady Whiteadder in Blackadder. *Dickens' Women* was created for the Edinburgh Festival of 1989, and was nominated for an Olivier Award in 1991. Her distinguished film career was crowned with a BAFTA Best Supporting Actress for *The Age of Innocence* in 1991, and she was awarded the OBE for her services to drama in 2001. Margolyes will be touring the world in 2012, celebrating in performance the bicentenary of Charles Dickens' birth.